Conversations with the Wise Uncle

Other Books by
Dennis E. Coates, Ph.D.

Conversations with the Wise Aunt (2012)

Adult Discussion Guides

Learning from the Wise Aunt (2012)

Learning from the Wise Uncle (2012)

Praise for
Conversations with the Wise Uncle

"Folksy story with a powerful message." – Bill Lampton, Ph.D., communication consultant and speech coach

"I would recommend it to every parent – or for that matter, every teenage boy." – Julie Walker, business consultant and mother of two

"Raising kids is not easy and I wish I had this book a few years ago." – James Palmer, author, expert on online newsletters and father of four

"I am putting into practice some of his advice and am grateful to read such a clear and loving voice." – Elizabeth Aquino, mother of three

"This book shows how to help give your child the tools to develop those critical life skills they need. This is a must read for all parents of teenagers." – Bruce Knight, career coach and father of three sons

"Coates has written a truly brilliant book. He has managed to fit into this short, easy read, dozens of critical life lessons such as: respecting women, thinking before you act, manners, being strong in the face of adversity, lifelong learning, the importance of giving, and the dangers of alcohol and drugs." – David J. Singer, author of *Six Simple Rules for a Better Life*

"Mr. Coates has crammed a lot of well-researched and thoughtful insight into fewer than 200 pages." – Ron Wilson, retired CLO

"The book has a place in our homes, schools, youth clubs, and church youth groups. I highly recommend it." – Roger Wenschlag, CEO of Performance Solutions

"Oh how much better prepared I would have been, for those challenging teen years, if only this book had been available then." – Clinton Whitehead, retired electrical engineer

"This is a good, thought provoking, and helpful book for any parent or youngster to read for some insight into life lessons better learned young than through bad decisions." – B. Hodges, retired executive chef and winemaker

Conversations with the Wise Uncle

*The Secret to Being Strong as a
Teenager and Preparing for Success as
an Adult*

Dennis E. Coates, Ph.D.

First Summit Publishing

Printed in the United States of America
First Summit Publishing
P.O. Box 1655
Newport News, VA 23601
757-873-3700

Cover photograph: Klaus-Peter Adler, Fotolia.com
Cover design and interior composition: Paula Schlauch
Sketches: Dennis E. Coates.
Library of Congress Cataloguing-in-Publication Data is available.

ISBN - 978-0-9850156-3-3

The places, characters and events portrayed in this story are completely fictional and have no relation to anyone living or dead—with the exception of Little Rock, which is a real city in Arkansas, and Habitat for Humanity, which is a real charitable institution with programs in many cities throughout the U.S.

It's a huge blessing for a teen boy to know adults who will give him a "heads-up" about life.

I've written this book to help make that happen.

CONTENTS

The Heads-Up Talk

This book exists because of a story my best friend told me.

When he was 12, his uncle took him out for breakfast. In addition to potatoes and eggs, they shared a long talk. His uncle was relaxed and fun to be with, not at all like his dad, who was stern, demanding and hard to talk to.

In a friendly, casual way, his uncle talked about what the boy could expect during his teen years. He described the physical changes that were about to happen to him as he matured into an adult. He talked about peer pressure, risk-taking behavior and the consequences of sex, drugs and alcohol.

At the end of the talk his uncle said, "Now I want you to promise me something. When your friends want you to go along with them and something inside you doesn't feel right, I want you to stop and think about what could happen. I want you to remember the things we talked about. Will you do that?"

My friend told me this talk with his uncle was the most important conversation of his life, that it helped him steer clear of all kinds of trouble during his teen years. Not that he was a perfect kid, whatever that is. But most of the time when he was tempted to do something he knew he shouldn't, and usually it was something fun or exciting, he remembered what his uncle told him. He said having an uncle who leveled with him about the consequences of bad decisions was the luckiest thing that ever happened to him.

Many adults don't feel comfortable talking to kids about these things. Why? Because there's so much ground to cover, and they know they're not experts on every topic. Besides, times have changed, and they remember their own teen years as a confusing time of life, a mixed bag of issues, anxiety and fun. So even caring adults may not have the confidence to say the right things. I've talked to quite a few people about their teen experiences, and my friend is the only person I've ever met who had anything like a "wise uncle" conversation.

It made me think of my own teen years. No one ever sat me down and explained things to me. My dad was always busy with work, and there were times he was away from home a lot. My mom had her hands full taking care of my younger brothers and sisters.

During junior high and high school a few adults took an interest in me—a scoutmaster, a wrestling coach, an English teacher, and an elder in my church. Later in life I was lucky to have a few colleagues and bosses who gave me advice.

The problem was, I didn't always get the coaching when I needed it, and there were huge gaps that I had to fill in on my own. Some of this learning came from mistakes. I'm still learning, but it would have been great to have some of this wisdom back when I was a teenager.

So I wish every young man could have the kind of "wise uncle" talk my friend had. A kid could avoid a lot of trouble and misery by hearing these insights at the right time. And the long-term benefits would be enormous.

If you're a teenager or approaching that age, maybe someone who cares about you gave you this book.

By now you probably no longer take everything that adults say as gospel. That's a good instinct, because nobody has all the answers. More important, not too long from now you'll be an adult, so you need to get used to thinking for yourself.

But it would be a mistake to dismiss everything adults tell you. As Mark Twain once wrote, "When I was a boy of fourteen, my father was so ignorant I could hardly stand to have the old man around. But when I got to be twenty-one, I was astonished at how much he had learned in seven years." It makes sense to listen, evaluate and judge for yourself how useful the input is.

It's a huge advantage to have relationships with caring adults who share what they know. Many kids aren't lucky enough to have a mentor like my friend's uncle. That's why I wrote this book. I created a fictional story of my friend's "wise uncle" conversation, added some of the coaching I've had over the years, and included some information I've learned since about teen brain development.

The story is about a young man named Chris and his uncle Ray, who live in Little Rock, Arkansas. It doesn't portray a single conversation, but several that take place during his teen years. These are the ideal "wise uncle" talks I never had, the way I wish they had happened.

And it isn't a long book. It doesn't include every conversation Chris and his uncle Ray would have had over the years.

Everybody's teen journey is different, so your own situation isn't exactly like Chris's. His life isn't your life. His dreams aren't the same as your dreams. The story may be about someone else, but the insights are about you.

So take them seriously. Look over Chris's shoulder while he learns things that many kids your age haven't been told. Grab Uncle Ray's insights and make the most of them. They'll help you avoid most of the perils of growing up, guide you to become strong as a man and give you a huge edge on life.

The Melon and the Ball of String

It was a hot Little Rock summer. Chris was 12 years old, and every Saturday morning at eight o'clock he'd ride his bike to his uncle Ray's house and mow his lawn. It was a big deal because he was saving up to buy a brand new set of golf clubs. He wanted the best clubs money could buy, which cost almost $2,000. He was too young to be hired for a regular job, so to make money he mowed lawns. Uncle Ray paid him twenty bucks to mow his lawn, and he let Chris use his mower and gas. Plus, he had introduced Chris to other people in the neighborhood who paid him to mow their lawns.

When he got to his uncle's house, Chris saw him sitting on the front porch with a cup of coffee. He was wearing an old white shirt and jeans. A bucket hat covered most of his curly brown hair. "Hey guy," he said. "You want some coffee?"

Chris loved it when his uncle offered him a cup of coffee. It made him feel grown up.

The two of them sat on the porch and looked out on the neighborhood. "Which lawns are you doing today?"

"Well, after yours I'll do Mrs. Henderson's, then the Bachmann's."

"Hoo! That's a lot of mowing. Can you get it all done by lunch?"

"Yeah, once I get going I don't stop."

"That's my guy. Hey, why don't you have lunch with me when you're done?"

"Okay. What are you doing today, Uncle Ray?"

"Today I'm going to start rebuilding my shed. The first step is to knock down the old one. I could use some help if you're up to it. I'll pay you."

"Okay." He knew he'd be tired after mowing three lawns, but he figured lunch would pick him up. He never said no to a chance to make some money.

"Where's your hat and gloves? Where's your sunglasses?"

Chris felt embarrassed. "I guess I left them at home." He was in a hurry to get started and besides, he didn't like wearing a hat.

"Well, you can't work in the hot sun without sunglasses. Here, take mine. I'll get you a hat and some gloves."

Uncle Ray was right. It gets hot in Arkansas in summer. When his uncle returned, he handed Chris a bottle of sunscreen. "Put some of that on, too."

Uncle Ray had a big lawn. Chris just put his head down and pushed the mower forward, row after row. The lawn sloped down in the back. Going down was easy, but he got some serious exercise coming back. He saw the old shed at the bottom of the slope. He thought it would be fun to take it down. Before long he was sweating up a storm.

Chris was the oldest of four children. As he pushed the mower he thought about his mom. Everyone said she was good at caring for young children. She could calm a crying baby—anybody's crying baby. She had a business designing and making custom jewelry. But Sunday was her favorite day of the week. She had a good singing voice and was the music director in church.

Neither his mom nor his dad graduated from college. His mom told him that when she was a teenager she ran away from home without finishing high school. His dad had a year of college. He was a manager at one of the big grocery stores in town.

Chris's dad loved playing golf, and he loved sports. Chris guessed that he got his own enthusiasm for sports from him. His dad studied military history and participated in a local re-enactment society. Because his father didn't like working with his hands, it was Uncle

Ray who taught Chris about tools. And it was Uncle Ray who got him into mowing lawns. He said it would get him in shape. He said that the key to beating his dad at golf was getting physically fit.

Chris thought about that as he pushed the mower, and he picked up the pace. When he finished, Uncle Ray was waiting for him with a big glass of ice water.

"Good job, Chris. Here, drink this. You're covered with sweat. You need to stay hydrated in this heat."

Later, after Chris had finished the other two lawns, he joined Uncle Ray in his kitchen. His uncle made great sandwiches. He called them "dagwoods," because the comic strip character Dagwood loved piled-high sandwiches. When Chris had cleaned up there were two tall sandwiches waiting on the kitchen table. He sat down and grabbed one.

Uncle Ray was pouring drinks. He smiled at Chris and said, "Hold on, partner. Wait for me. You don't start eating until everyone's at the table. It's considered a courtesy. You know why?"

"No, why?"

"Guess."

He thought about it. "So everything's equal?"

"Well, that's the spirit. Imagine you're me, getting lunch ready. If I started eating without you, how would you feel? If you wait until I'm at the table, it shows you care about me."

"I get it."

Uncle Ray joined him at the table. "You're a quick learner, all right."

The two of them dug into the sandwiches. When they were done, Uncle Ray said, "Well, Chris, do you feel like helping me with the shed out back?"

"Yeah!"

"Great. We'll have some fruit and then go out back." He went to the refrigerator and retrieved a large cantaloupe. Then he opened a drawer, pulled out a knife, a ball of string, and a magic marker.

He handed Chris the melon. "Smell it," he said.

It had a wonderful sweet smell.

"That's how you can tell when a melon is going to taste great. If it smells great, it'll taste great. If it doesn't smell like much, it's not ready and it won't have much flavor."

"Hmm."

"Before we dig in, I want to tell you something important."

"Okay." Chris wondered what it could be. He thought it might have something to do with the shed.

Uncle Ray began drawing a face on the melon. It was a pretty good face. He didn't know Uncle Ray could draw. He drew some hair on top and gave the face a smile.

"There," he said. "This is you."

Chris laughed. "It doesn't look like me."

Then his uncle gave him the ball of string. "Here, hold this while I pull out some of the string." He measured a length as wide as his fist, and made a knot there. Then he measured another fist-width and made another knot. He continued doing this until he made ten knots. Then he cut the string with the knife.

"Do you know how old Alexander is?" he asked.

Alexander was a dachshund, Chris's dog. "We've always had him. I guess he's as old as I am."

"Maybe a little less. I think your folks got him after you were born. Let's say he's ten years old."

"Okay."

Uncle Ray stretched the knotted string across the length of the table. "Dachshunds live to be about 15 years." He took the marker and made a mark halfway between the first knot and the second knot. "Think of the string as a hundred years. Right here is where Alexander is today. So you can see that if he stays healthy, he has at least five more years. Do you know why they named him Alexander?"

"Because of Alexander the Great?"

"That's right. Your dad probably told you that Alexander was a brilliant Greek general a couple hundred years before the time of Christ. He commanded armies when he was a teenager not much older than you are. His armies went way beyond Greece and conquered every opposing force. His empire was huge, the largest ever in ancient times. Even today, 2,500 years later, the U.S. Army studies his tactics to learn how he did it."

"Wow. Dad was in the Army before he met Mom. He's been interested in wars and stuff ever since. That's probably why he named our dog Alexander."

"I bet you're right. Alexander's a wonderful companion, isn't he?"

"Yeah. He's my buddy."

"Appreciate him and love him all you can every day, Chris. Because dogs don't live forever. We have them and we cherish them just like family, and eventually their time is up. They pass away, just like people do."

It made Chris a little sad to think about it. He felt uncomfortable talking about Alexander this way.

"We need to appreciate your Grandpa and Grandma every day, too. They're in their mid-sixties." He marked this on the string. "The average person lives 80 or 85 years. But your grandparents could live a lot longer. Lots of people live to be 90. Some live to be 100. Maybe you'll live to be 100, Chris." All this was plainly visible on the string. He saw that Grandma and Grandpa had quite a bit more time left.

"Right now, I'm 38 years old," he said, and marked the string again, just short of the forty-year knot.

Then Uncle Ray said, "And this is you, right here." He made a mark just past the ten-year knot. "You've got a long life ahead of you, partner."

"Yeah."

"Part of the reason Alexander the Great was so successful was that he had a great teacher. His teacher was Aristotle, one of the greatest philosophers who ever lived. Man, was Alexander lucky!"

Chris smiled.

"I guess that makes me your Aristotle, doesn't it? Since I'm always showing you how to do stuff."

"Are you going to teach me how to be a general?"

"I don't know about that. But you're almost a teenager now, and I want to explain some important things to you."

Chris's heart started to beat faster. He wondered what his uncle had in mind.

"Let's start with this string." As Uncle Ray spoke, he marked the string. "When you finish high school you'll be 18, right about here. If you to go to college, that will take four more years, which will put you right about here, age 22. By then hopefully you'll know what you want to do in life. Maybe you'll be an electrician or a businessman. Or a lawyer or an engineer. Maybe you'll go to graduate school. Who knows? If you did, that would take another two or three years. After college, you'll start your career, earning good money. See? You're not even thirty years old yet."

He moved his hand past the third knot. "After a while, you might meet a great woman and get married. And like your parents, you might have kids of your own."

"I don't know what I want to do when I grow up."

"It's hard to say what you'll end up doing or what kind of career you'll have. But you still have a lot of time to figure that out, as you can see. Eventually, you'll retire, just as I hope to do about 20 or 30 years from now. By then, you'll be older than I am now. And later your own kids will get older and maybe they'll have kids, which would make you a grandpa yourself. So you see, Chris, you could have a great life. A long life."

Chris didn't know what to say. He didn't know why his uncle was telling him all this.

Then Uncle Ray put his finger just past the first knot. "But here's where you are now. Right here, at the beginning of your teen years. Even though you have your whole life ahead of you, the time when you're a teenager is probably the most important time you'll ever have. Did you know that?"

"What's so important about it? All the good stuff happens later."

His uncle chuckled. "That's right. A lot of good stuff does happen later. But a lot of really important stuff is about to happen for you real soon, and I want you to know about it."

"Like what, Uncle Ray?"

"Well for starters, you've been a boy for twelve years, going on thirteen."

"Uh huh."

"And your body is about to grow into a man's body."

"I'd like that."

Uncle Ray smiled, and then he put his hand on top of the cantaloupe. He patted it as he spoke.

"Your brain has a kind of biological clock in it, and the alarm is about to go off. That will trigger some chemicals, called hormones, to travel throughout your body. Growth hormones. It won't happen overnight, but your face is going to change into a man's face, your voice is going to change, and you'll probably grow a lot taller. Eventually, you'll have a man's body. And you'll feel like a man, too. You won't feel like a boy anymore."

Chris imagined a bigger version of himself. "That's fine with me."

"Growing up to be a man takes time. And to be a successful man takes hard work, like becoming a good athlete. And part of what makes it hard is that in addition to changes in your body, there's going to be changes in your brain."

Chris looked at him. He had no idea what he was talking about.

"Son, what I'm about to say is the most important thing I'll ever tell you."

Chris was a little nervous. He wondered what his uncle had in mind.

"Life is a joy, but it can also be difficult, dangerous and unforgiving. You're a boy now, and soon you'll be growing into a man. That means you're going to start making your own decisions. But the part of your brain that analyzes and makes decisions is about to enter a major growth phase."

"My brain is going to get bigger?"

"Not bigger. Smarter. Here, you see this melon guy? I want you to imagine that inside the top half of the melon is his brain. You've probably seen a drawing or a picture of a brain."

"Yeah."

"So you know your brain is really complicated. It's a lot like a computer, but way more powerful than any computer on Earth. Every part of your brain works as a system to help you think. Everything you do, everything you say, everything you think is triggered by your brain. It's what makes you smart."

"Right."

"Well, when you were born, you already had a complete brain. But the billions of tiny brain cells weren't connected up yet. It was like having a brand new computer with no software. As a baby, you learned to crawl by trying hard to crawl. You learned to walk by trying hard to walk. The same with learning how to talk, and so on. You learned all this by doing it. And all this effort caused your brain cells to physically wire together. You were programming your brain. Are you with me?"

"I think so."

"Good. Well, there's one part of your brain that won't get wired until you're a teenager."

"What's that?"

He placed the palm of his hand on his forehead. "It's this part right here. The last part of your brain to get wired is the part that makes you an exceptional learner, a logical thinker and a good decision-maker. Starting now and for about a dozen years, the connections you use here will become hard-wired. The ones you don't use will slowly wither away. All the other areas of your brain were constructed the same way. The brain cells that fire together will wire together, so it's use it or lose it. By the time you're in your early 20s, your basic foundation for critical thinking and decision-making will be set—for the rest of your life. If you spend the next ten years asking why and learning what causes what, your critical thinking ability will be huge. If all you do is have fun, fool around and do dumb things, it will be small. It's totally up to you."

"Will I stop learning after I grow up?"

"No. You can keep on learning until the day you die. The question is, how easy will it be for you to learn, to think well, and make good decisions? Think of your ability to learn and the knowledge you'll gain as a house. If during adolescence you lay down a large foundation, you can build a large house on it. If you make a small foundation, then later as an adult you can only build a small house on it. Right now is the time when you start building this foundation. After you're a fully grown man, you'll have to live with whatever foundation you constructed during high school and college."

"But Uncle Ray, how can I get more brain cells connected?"

"All you have to do is exercise that part of the brain as often as you can. Be a questioner. Try to understand what's going on in the world and why. Be someone who asks 'why' and 'what if' questions about everything. Why did this happen? How does this work? What if I try something different? Doing this will train your brain to think. So if you want to grow up smart, you've got to be Mr. Curiosity."

"I don't think I'll have a problem with that. I'm already curious. I'm always asking questions about everything."

"I know you are. Keep doing that, Chris. What happens to you along the rest of the knots in the string depends on it. The more you ask, the more you learn. The more you learn, the more you understand. You want to build the biggest possible platform for understanding. And there's one more way you can do that. It's actually the most important way."

"What's that?"

"The trick is to ask yourself, 'If I do this, what will happen?' Say that back to me, Chris."

"If I do this, what will happen?"

"Right. You ask yourself that, and then you imagine the consequences. Be conscious that you're about to make a choice, and that you're in charge of the choices you make. Will you promise me you'll always try to do that?"

"Sure, Uncle Ray. I promise."

"And if you feel the consequences are going to be bad, then don't go there."

"So before I do something, I think ahead. Think about what might happen if I do it."

"Exactly. And every time you do that, you'll be programming the front part of your brain."

For a few moments, Chris and his uncle looked at each other without speaking. Then Ray said, "And there's another reason for doing that."

"It'll help me stay out of trouble."

"That's exactly right, Chris. You'll be amazed at some of the dumb and dangerous things your friends are going to want to do in the years ahead. You'll be tempted to go along, because maybe they'll feel you don't belong if you don't. But some of them are going to get hurt, and some of them are going to get in trouble, and you don't want to be a part of it."

"Maybe it's not a good idea to have friends like that."

"That's a good point. And Chris, there's another reason why doing the right thing isn't always going to be so easy. With the front part of your brain under construction, sometimes it won't be so easy to think things through logically and make the right decision. You'll have good intentions, but you'll feel like acting impulsively and reacting emotionally instead. Which is what teenagers often do."

"So what am I supposed to do?"

"Good question. You'll have two things going for you. First, you already know you need to ask 'why' and 'what if' questions. You know you need to think about consequences. Knowing you need to do this will actually help you do it. And also, I'll help you. I'll be your Aristotle."

"All right!"

"Other adults can help, too. A good teacher can help you ponder and analyze while you're learning. If you make the golf team, your coach can help you think about golf strategy. Your dad can help you solve problems, if you let him. And your mom. You're lucky to have such great parents, Chris. The key is to take what they say seriously. Don't blow them off just because they're not telling you what you want to hear."

"I want to be smart like you."

Uncle Ray laughed. "You'll end up smarter than I am. I guarantee it."

Chris wondered if his uncle was right. The idea that he could be that smart made him feel great.

"Now let's eat this cantaloupe and go tear down the shed."

—————————— ❖ ——————————

"The last part of your brain to get wired is the part that makes you an exceptional learner, a logical thinker and a good decision-maker. Starting now and for about a dozen years, the connections you use here will become hard-wired. The ones you don't use will slowly wither away. All the other areas of your brain were constructed the same way. The brain cells that fire together will wire together, so it's use it or lose it. By the time you're in your early 20s, your basic foundation for critical thinking and decision-making will be set—for the rest of your life. If you spend the next ten years asking why and learning what causes what, your critical thinking ability will be huge. If all you do is have fun, fool around and do dumb things, it will be small. It's totally up to you."

—————————— ❖ ——————————

The Onion and the Full Plate

The old shed, which had a plywood floor on top of concrete blocks, was fairly easy to tear down. With the two of them working together, the project took only an hour. The clean-up took another hour.

The next Saturday, the two of them poured a foundation for the new shed, which was delivered later that week as a kit. The following Saturday afternoon, Chris and his uncle were on the front porch talking about the new shed.

Uncle Ray pointed at a diagram on the instructions. "You know those braces we set in the concrete?"

"Yeah?"

"According to this, each corner has a support, which attaches to a brace. The walls attach to the supports. Looks like the roof goes on last."

"Yeah."

"Okay, you be in charge of staging. You organize the parts so you can hand them to me for the next step."

"Okay."

Chris discovered that his job was pretty easy. Before long he had all the parts organized on the ground in step sequence.

"Hey, it looks like you're way ahead of me. Why don't you grab that wrench and do the opposite wall the way I'm doing this one. You know how that wrench works?"

"I think so. You just get the right socket and plug it in."

"Right. See what I'm doing here? You use these big nuts and screw on the bolts. You finger-tighten them until they're all in place, then you go back and tighten them all as hard as you can with the wrench."

"Got it."

After about an hour, Uncle Ray said. "Let's take a break. It's hot out here, and I'm craving some iced tea."

Inside, they sat at the kitchen table. "We made great progress, didn't we? If we hit it for another hour or so, I think we can finish. You up for it?"

"Sure."

"You're getting good with those tools."

"I like working with tools."

"You think you'd like working on a construction crew?"

"I don't know."

"The money can be decent. You have to be physically strong, though. You seem to be a lot stronger than you used to be."

"It's because I've been pushing that lawn mower."

"Ha! Well, Chris, I tell you what. If you keep helping me with these projects, in a couple years you'll have some good construction skills. Then, if you like, I can talk to a builder friend of mine."

"That sounds great."

"You know, working with tools is a special area of learning. I think of it as one of the life skills."

"Life skills?"

"Well, there are all kinds of things you can learn that will help you make your way through life. You can survive without them, but life's a lot easier when you have the right skills. You can see how helpful it is when you know how to use tools."

"That's for sure."

"But there's more to life than using tools, like knowing what to eat and drink, and what not to. So you keep your body strong and healthy. How to use a computer. How to drive a car. How to work out in a gym. How to lift weights without hurting yourself. First aid."

"We have a first aid kit in the house and in the car. Dad showed me how to use it."

"That's great, Chris. I also think of manners and etiquette as life skills. They help you get along with people. In life, there's not much you can do if you don't know how to get along with people."

"I mow lawns all by myself."

"Good point. That's a good example of something you can do all by yourself. Another is cooking, a great life skill. You do any cooking at home?"

"No, mom does that."

"Well, your Uncle Ray does his own cooking. You know, since your Aunt Rachel got cancer and passed away. She was a great partner. I guess she spoiled me. Maybe someday you'll get married."

"Maybe."

Uncle Ray opened the pantry door and retrieved an onion. Then he picked up a knife from the counter and handed it to Chris. "Talking about life skills made me think of this onion. I want you to cut this onion into two pieces. Slice it right down the middle, right here."

"Okay."

When the onion was in two pieces, Uncle Ray picked up one of them.

"You see, this onion here is like you and me. It's got layers. We've got layers, too. We go through life, and we learn stuff. Every time we learn something important, it's like adding to the layers. What we learn becomes a part of us. Like learning how to use tools. What we learn adds thickness to the layers."

"So the layers in the onion represent what we learn."

"Exactly. And if you're lucky, you never stop learning."

His uncle put the onion in front of him. "You can see this onion has six layers, including the core. Think of the first three layers as kinds of learning that you and everybody else are pretty familiar with. I'll mention those first."

He pointed the knife at the outer layer. "You see this ring on the outside? Think of this one as knowledge and skills you need for your career. For example, if you end up being a lawyer, then this is what you need to know to practice law. If you're a doctor, like a surgeon or a dentist, then it represents medical know-how. If you become an Army officer, then it represents how to lead soldiers into combat. If you become an electrician, then this outer layer represents the know-how of that trade."

"So if I want to be a professional golfer, this would be everything I should know about golf."

"You got it. But there's a whole lot more you need to know to be successful."

"Like what?"

He pointed the knife at the second layer. "Let's call this next layer your formal education, the stuff you're learning now, and later in high school and college. Some of your education may help in your career, but most of it is pretty general. Your knowledge of history, literature, writing, math, art and science teaches you how the world works. Basic stuff. Business know-how comes later, when you get into your career."

Chris pointed at the onion. "So this is what I learn later, in my job. And the next ring is what I learn in school."

"Right."

"Uncle Ray?"

"What?"

"Some of the stuff they make us learn in school is so boring. It doesn't seem to have to do with anything."

"Which ones are boring?"

"Like history."

"Yes, history can be boring, especially if your teacher only tells you what happened and not why it happened. But learning why the good things and bad things in history happened can be fun. Even exciting."

"Well, Mr. Crowder is boring."

"I'm sorry to hear it. But you know what?"

"What?"

"You shouldn't blame Mr. Crowder."

"Why not? He's the teacher. It's his job to make us learn."

"Do you really think somebody can make you learn? If you decided you didn't care about a subject and you weren't going to make the effort, what could a teacher do to force you to learn it anyway?"

Chris thought about that for a moment. "I don't know."

"The truth is, no one can make you learn. And no one can keep you from learning. If you're really interested or if you make up your mind to master something, nobody can stop you. When it comes to learning, you're in charge, not the teacher."

"I never thought of it that way."

"Chris, you're going to have some wonderful teachers, and you're going to have some who are, well, boring. And everything in between. The students who come out on top are those who just accept it and learn anyway."

"But why should I learn stuff I don't care about? Stuff I'm never going to use?"

"Do you remember when we talked about developing the smart part of your brain by asking why and what if questions?"

"Sure."

"So here's a why question for you. Why should you go ahead and learn the history of cause and effect, and for that matter any other subject they might put in front of you?"

Chris gave that some thought. Then he said, "I guess maybe I'll probably end up needing to know some of this stuff, even if I can't imagine it right now."

"That's good. Can you think of an example?"

Chris frowned. "Nothing comes to mind right now."

"Okay. How about this. Someday you'll be old enough to vote. One candidate will promise he'll do certain things. The other candidate will promise something totally different. Sound familiar?"

"Yeah..."

"Well, which one would you support? You'd need to understand the consequences of each plan. The examples of history are how you learn that."

"Maybe so."

"Can you think of any other reasons for learning things you think are boring?"

"Maybe these are just things I ought to know, whether they're fun or not."

"Good point. You need to know about the world you live in. Once you're an adult and on your own, you either get what's going on or you're clueless. It's not really about becoming a mathematician or an expert in history. It's about understanding how the world works."

"Yeah."

"But I can think of another, even more important reason to learn something like history. It's because understanding the events of history makes you think. It forces you to think logically. It's as if the history itself isn't actually as important as what learning it does to your brain. It makes you a better thinker."

"Hmm."

"So, Chris, don't let your teacher hold you back. Take whatever you can from Mr. Crowder and do the rest yourself. Take responsibility for your own learning. Learn it anyway. Get your A anyway."

"Gosh, that was some pep talk!"

"I told you I was going to be your Aristotle."

Uncle Ray moved the knife to the next ring. He smiled and said, "This ring represents life skills, what we were talking about before. Most of this stuff you don't learn in school. Using tools, operating machines, organizing a work space, safe driving, managing your money. How to dress and take care of your clothes. I could go on and on. There are a ton of life skills. Speaking of managing your money, how are you doing saving up for your golf clubs?"

"I have about four hundred dollars. It's not enough for what I want."

"Where is this money?"

"I keep it in a box in my drawer."

"Did you know that if you keep it in a bank, they'll not only make sure it's safe, they'll actually pay you a little extra for keeping it there?"

"Really? How much would they pay me?"

"Where you keep the money is called a savings account. What they pay you is called interest. The more you put into your account, the more they pay you. For example, if you have a thousand dollars in your account, after a year they'll add ten bucks or so to it, depending on the interest rate. It can add up. If you want, your mom and dad will help you open it."

"Dad said I ought to get one."

"Making your money grow is a life skill. There are other ways besides a savings account. They don't teach you this in school, but it's important."

"Yeah."

"Let me tell you a story about a life skill I learned. When I was in high school, I had this girl friend. Her name was Sandy. She was smart, and I thought I was in love. Anyway, one day she and I took a walk in the park. We took our shoes and socks off and walked around in the grass barefoot. Then we sat under a tree and talked all afternoon. It was great. About the time I thought it would be nice to kiss her, she said she had to get back. I was putting on my socks when she said I wasn't doing it right. She explained how you're supposed to put your socks on so they last longer. I guess her mother taught her that, and now she was teaching me. Instead of romance, I got a lesson in putting my socks on the right way."

"That's funny."

"I didn't think it was funny at the time, but you know what? I still put my socks on that way—the way she showed me."

"Did she teach you anything else?"

"Come to think of it, I think she did. She was very practical. We lost touch after we left high school. It's a good thing we didn't stay together. I don't think we would have made a good couple."

"Why not?"

"Well, I wasn't ready. There was a lot I didn't know. I wish I had learned more when I was a teenager. I had a lot of catching up to do later in life."

"Uncle Ray?"

"Yes?"

"If they don't teach us life skills in school, and if there are a ton of them, how am I supposed to learn all that?"

"That's such a good question. The answer is, it takes a long time to learn the life skills you're going to need. You just accept that you need to work on it and you go after one skill at a time. Some people grow up with very few life skills. In a way, they're handicapped. So if you start acquiring these skills as a teenager, it puts you way ahead of the game."

"Okay."

Uncle Ray tapped the face of the onion with the knife. "So it's typical for people to acquire business know-how, basic education and life skills – the outer three rings. Your world is set up fairly well to help you in these areas, if you seek it. But the next three layers – the inner ones – are not consciously taught in most families, schools or businesses. You and I are going to concentrate on them on our own, because they're even more important than the other three. For example, this next layer here is about critical thinking skills."

"What's that?"

"Remember when we talked about problem-solving and decision-making, the front part of your brain that's under construction?"

"Yeah."

"That's what I'm talking about—your ability to do higher level thinking. Not just understanding how things work, but why. Figuring out what causes what. Analyzing a situation and choosing the best way to act. Solving a problem. Imagining future consequences. Coming up with a plan of action."

"Right. You said you were going to help me."

"What I plan to do is coach you—to think for yourself as we do things together. You learn to think by thinking, just as you get better at golf by playing golf."

"I get it."

"There are two more layers that are not consciously addressed with young people. This next ring has to do with knowing how to relate to people. It's called people skills. It's the skills involved in communicating with others. How to listen, how to keep an open mind when someone is talking to you, how to resolve a conflict, how to praise and encourage people, how to tell someone when you don't like what they're doing. Because if you don't deal with these situations right, things don't go well. The truth is, a lot of people have trouble with people skills, because they aren't taught in schools."

"Why not?"

"Beats me. I think they should be. They're important in every aspect of life where people are involved—school, friendships, work, family, marriage—virtually everything. Adults who have good people skills rise quickly in their careers. It's a game-changer, Chris."

"Are you going to teach me some people skills, Uncle Ray?"

"I can coach you. Actually, I'm still catching up in this department myself, after all these years.

"Well it looks like we've run out of rings. All that's left is the core. I think of this area here, right smack in the middle of the onion, as being strong as a person."

"You mean working out?"

"It is a lot like working out. Only instead of physical strength, you work on inner strength. Having strong character."

Chris thought about that. He liked the idea of being strong. But he wasn't sure what his uncle meant by "being strong as a person."

"You know how doing the right thing almost always means doing the hard thing? Like telling the truth when the truth is embarrassing? Or being patient when you're in a hurry? Or staying focused on a task or getting your homework done when you'd rather be having fun? This is what is called personal strength, being strong as a person."

"Am I strong as person?"

"I think you are, Chris, in many ways. For example, instead of goofing off, you're mowing lawns and helping me build a shed. That takes focus. And effort. And commitment and patience. It would be a whole lot easier to just fool around and have fun."

"But I like to have fun."

"And you should. Life should be fun. But life is also challenging, and it takes strength to get through the tough times. Most things worth having don't come easy."

"Friends are worth having, and making friends is easy."

"I'm sure it is for you. But having a best friend takes effort, and keeping friends over the years isn't so easy, as you'll find out. But you're right. Some good things are easy. Like appreciating nature, for example. But for some reason, you have to work like crazy to get most things worth having. I'm not sure why that is, but it's true."

"I've been working hard to buy some new golf clubs, and I still don't have enough."

"But you're still working at it. You haven't given up. It takes strength to persevere. Another strength you have is you work on yourself. Not every kid does that."

"I want to get really good at golf."

"I know. And every time you learn something it makes you stronger. There's a lot to learn." He held up the onion. "So you see why these three inner layers—personal strengths, people skills and critical thinking skills—are really important to your success. Think about it, Chris. If you aren't strong deep inside, if you don't have courage, if you can't keep your cool, if you can't accept the truth, if you don't stay optimistic—in other words, if you don't do the hard things in life, then the rest of this stuff won't count for much. If you aren't good with people, you won't have good relationships, either in life or in your work. If you can't think straight and make good decisions, what good is everything else?"

Chris nodded. "I guess I have a lot to learn."

"Everyone does. I can tell you that when I went into the Army, I was way behind the learning curve. In fact, I'm still learning, still adding to my layers of ability. But you've got time. The more you learn while you're a teenager, the easier it's going to be for you later. Start now, get a head start, and you'll have a huge advantage when you're grown up. Many kids waste their teen years."

Uncle Ray got up from the table, opened a cabinet and pulled out a plate. He put it on the table and began taking the onion apart, starting with the core. He put each layer on the plate, one at a time.

"You've got a full plate, Chris. That's what we say when someone has a lot to do, and it seems like more than the average person can manage."

"It seems like a lot."

"It is. But there's one thing on this plate that's more important than anything else. It's so important that you should consciously start working on it, because you'll need to keep learning and growing until the day you die. You know what it is?"

"The front part of my brain?"

"Well yes, critical thinking skills are terribly important, but I'd make that number two. To me, the most important area of your development is the core of the onion. It's who you are as a person. Your character. Personal strengths. There are dozens of ways to be strong as a person, and if you make them your habit, it will be easier for you to do the right things, the hard things in life."

"I want to be strong. I want to be good at doing stuff."

"You can and you will. In my opinion, you're off to a great start. I've told you things most kids never hear. And I know other people who can help you. We're not going to wait until you're grown up."

"Thanks, Uncle Ray."

"You bet. We're going to keep you ahead of the learning curve, Chris."

— ❖ —

A Teen's Full Plate of Learning

In addition to life skills
and formal education...

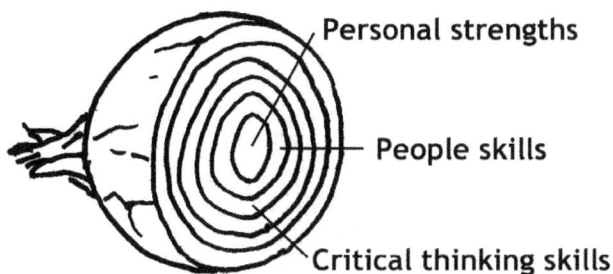

Personal strengths

People skills

Critical thinking skills

— ❖ —

————————— ❖ —————————

"The truth is, no one can make you learn. And no one can keep you from learning. If you're really interested or if you make up your mind to master something, nobody can stop you. When it comes to learning, you're in charge, not the teacher."

————————— ❖ —————————

Kissing in the Bushes

During the fall of Chris's eighth grade year, he got in trouble at school.

One of his teachers caught him and a girl named Monica making out behind some bushes during recess. He guessed one of the other kids saw them and told a teacher, who sent them to the vice principal's office. She gave Chris detention and notified his mother.

His mother was not pleased. "I want to hear your side of this."

"She's just a friend, Mom. Her name is Monica."

"Your girl friend. What were you doing in the bushes?"

"We were just kissing."

"Kissing. On school grounds."

"I didn't know it was such a crime."

"Well, it may not be a crime, but it's a violation of the PDA rule. Now you have a black mark at school."

"You're not going to tell Dad, are you?"

"Well, that depends on you. Did you learn your lesson?"

"Yes."

"Tell me it's never going to happen again."

"It won't ever happen again, Mom. Please don't tell Dad. He doesn't need to know."

"Okay. This time."

And that was that. His mom never brought up the incident again.

But the next Saturday, before Chris started mowing, Uncle Ray took him to their favorite pancake house for breakfast. After the waitress brought their coffee, his uncle said, "Your mom told me about Monica."

"Oh great. Mom said she wouldn't tell anyone."

"She said she promised not to tell your dad. You can count on me not tell him. But she asked me to talk to you about it."

Chris wondered who else she told.

"Chris, this kissing business isn't a big scandal in my book. But I'd like to talk about it a little, if that's all right with you."

"What's there to talk about?"

"Not much. The truth is, kissing is nice, but sitting in detention is not. Remember I told you when I agreed to be your coach that it would be my job to help you ask why and what if questions? That's all I want to do. I just want to exercise the analysis and decision-making part of your brain a little."

Chris looked down at the table.

"What actually happened?"

"Monica and I are friends. She likes to kiss."

"How come you got reported?"

"We were in the bushes at the other end of the playing field at school. We'd been there before and nothing ever happened. I think some kid told on us."

"Why do you think the school made such a big deal out of it?"

"I don't know. Why is kissing such a big deal?"

"Actually, I think kissing is nice. Try this, Chris. Imagine that you're the vice-principal. Why do you think she was upset?"

"I have no idea."

"Think about it. What do you think was going on in her mind?"

"How should I know? Maybe she thought we were doing something else."

"Like what?"

"I don't know. Like sex maybe."

"You think she thought the kissing would lead to sex?"

Chris didn't even know what sex was like. He'd imagined it, and the thought was exciting. "Uncle Ray, all we wanted to do was make out."

"Is it possible your vice principal was worried that kissing is an emotional thing and the two of you could get carried away? If not this time, then sometime in the future?"

Chris hadn't thought about that. They hadn't done anything wrong. But if they got excited, maybe they'd want to do more.

"Maybe."

"Also, maybe your principal doesn't like students making out on school grounds. Can you imagine why?"

"No."

"Guess."

"Do we have to talk about this?"

"I'll give you a hint. What if the kids talked about it and word got to their parents. Who do you think the parents would come after? You or the vice principal?"

"I guess they'd call her."

"Why do you think parents might be upset, even if their kid wasn't involved?"

"I don't know."

"What if the parents got worried about what might happen?"

"You mean if their own kids did what we did?"

"Right. If that sort of thing is allowed to go on at school, then maybe their own kids might want to try it, too."

Chris was silent for a while. He was upset about the whole thing. He had to go to the vice principal's office, and his friends were asking him about it. They called his mother and made him do detention. Even though only kissing was involved, he had to admit that parents might worry about it anyway. Some of his friends claimed they'd had sex with girls.

"Uncle Ray, did you have sex when you were a teenager?"

"I wanted to, I have to admit. But no, I didn't know much about it. I thought if I tried, maybe the girl would be offended or something. So no, I didn't have sex until I was an adult."

"Do you think it's wrong to have sex?"

"No, Chris. Sex is natural. A good thing. A wonderful thing, actually. But it's risky. Sex has some big-time consequences."

"What do you mean, risky?"

"Well, Chris, it's like kissing. People do it because they like each other and want to be close to each other, and it feels good. But let's talk about this for a second, because you need to understand the risks. What do you think might happen if you had sex with a girl?"

"I guess she could get pregnant."

"Right. Tell me why that's a big deal."

"They might make her leave school. I've never seen a pregnant girl at school."

"What else?"

"Well, she'd have a baby."

"Is that a good thing or a bad thing, Chris?"

"Bad, I guess."

"Why?"

"Because then she'd have to take care of it."

"Of course she'd have to take care of it. But wouldn't the guy who got her pregnant help her?"

"I guess so."

"Chris. If you had sex with a girl, and if she got pregnant, and if she had a baby, who would the father be?"

Wow, Chris thought. *I'd be the father.*

"Do you want to be a father, Chris?"

"No. Not now, anyway."

"Why not?"

"I'm too young, Uncle Ray! I'm supposed to play golf and get good grades and stuff. Not take care of a kid."

"So you're saying these are consequence you want to avoid. That would be a pretty awful scenario, wouldn't it? Would you marry the girl?"

"Uncle Ray, I'm only thirteen. I'm too young to get married and be a father."

"You're right. Ten years from now you might still be too young to be a father. It's a huge responsibility that changes your whole life. Having sex with a young girl and getting her pregnant is one of the worst things that could happen to you as a teenager. And to her."

Chris tried to imagine Monica taking care of a baby. It would be just as bad for her as it would be for him. And he couldn't imagine getting married to her.

"And something else. As bad as it is, if you got a girl pregnant, there are even worse consequences than if she had a baby."

"Like what?"

"Well, her parents might convince her not to have the baby. They might want her to get an abortion. Do you know what an abortion is?"

"Not exactly."

"Well, it's when a doctor makes the fetus come out before it becomes a baby. If they try to do it early enough they might use drugs. Or if they wait too long, they might have to do it surgically. Basically they terminate what would have been a human being. You and your friend might have regrets about that for the rest of your life. And it's expensive. It's not something you want your friend to have to go through."

"Wow."

"For that matter, it's expensive to give birth. And it's a hundred times more expensive to raise a child. If you were a 13-year-old father, how would you pay for all that? Somebody would have to pay."

Chris was having trouble imagining all this. He didn't know what any of it cost.

"And that's not all," said his uncle. "She might carry the child for nine months and the baby could be born dead. Sometimes if there are complications, even the mother can die while giving birth. Your friend Monica could die, Chris. I'm not trying to scare you, but this is serious business. It's cause and effect in the real world. The risks are real. Huge. It's silly to be fooling around with sex when you don't know what the consequences are."

"I guess so."

"And there's something else to think about. If your friend has already had sex with someone else, her other partner could have given her a sexually transmitted disease, like HIV. HIV can kill you."

"I know."

"Or gonorrhea, or syphilis, or chlamydia, or herpes. She could infect you. You could get painful sores on your penis. If you didn't get it treated right away, it could get a lot worse."

Chris didn't know what to say. He hadn't thought about this before. His friends always talked about sex as something cool.

"Chris."

"Yeah."

"You think about sex sometimes, don't you?"

"Sure."

"Probably a lot more than when you were younger, right?"

"I guess so."

"It's natural and healthy to feel sexual desire. One of the changes that's happening in your body now that you're a teenager is the presence of the hormone testosterone. The more testosterone you have in your body, the stronger the urge to have sex. It's biology. This is true for both men and women. Your body is maturing and that's why you think more about sex now."

"Do girls think about sex, too?"

"Yes, they do. But the difference is that boys have about ten times as much testosterone as girls."

"Wow!"

"Do you know what this means?"

"No, what?"

"It means that boys think differently about sex than girls do. Usually, it's the boy who pushes the girl to have sex. It puts her in a bad position. She may want to say no, but feel pressured to say yes. If she gives in, that's when bad things can happen."

"Monica was the one who wanted me to kiss her."

"She probably likes you a lot. And I think kissing is really nice, especially when two people like each other. And when it's not on school grounds."

"Right."

"You like Monica, don't you?"

"Sure."

"I want to tell you something important about sex, Chris."

"What's that?"

"When a boy feels sexual urges, he might want to talk the girl into going beyond kissing. He might feel it so strongly he fails to think of the consequences. Hopefully, she will stand her ground. But Chris..."

"What, Uncle Ray?"

"Chris, if you really care about the girl, if you really have feelings for her..."

"Yes?"

"You'll respect her feelings. You won't put her in that position. Even if you really want to have sex, you won't make her draw the line. You'll respect her and not push her to get carried away."

"I wouldn't do that, Uncle Ray. I don't want any trouble."

"You have a good spirit, Chris. Sex will happen for you later, at the right time. It's a wonderful thing, one of the best things you'll ever experience in life. But because of the risks, it's smart to wait until you're a mature adult and ready to have a fully committed love relationship, like marriage."

"Uncle Ray?"

"What?"

"I don't think we need to talk about this anymore. I'm not ready to have sex with anybody. I'm not ready to deal with it now. I've got a full plate of stuff I want to do."

"I think your mom was worried because this is a danger area. But you're going to be fine. When you get tempted to go too far with a girl, you'll use the smart part of your brain. The part that makes you think before you act. The part that understands the risks and the consequences. The part that says 'no' when your emotions say 'yes.'"

———————— ❖ ————————

"Ten years from now you might still be too young to be a father. It's a huge responsibility that changes your whole life. Having sex with a young girl and getting her pregnant is one of the worst things that could happen to you as a teenager. And to her."

———————— ❖ ————————

The Game Between the Ears

It was April of the following year, and Chris was at his uncle's house, playing a video game in front of the TV in the living room. His uncle walked in and said, "You winning?"

The images on the screen made it seem like the viewer was going from room to room. An evil-looking character appeared, Chris pushed buttons on the controller, and the villain was blown to bloody bits. "I'm trying to make it to the next level."

"Well here you go, partner. Happy Birthday." Uncle Ray handed him a wrapped gift box. "Now that you're fourteen, I thought you could use this."

Chris turned off the TV, quickly unwrapped the box, and opened it. "Wow," he said. "A razor. Wow. I don't have one, but I've been thinking about getting one."

"Your Dad gave me the idea for it. Time to start shaving that fuzz off. I figured you should start with the latest model. In the bottom of the box are three cans of gel and enough spare blades to last you a year, at least."

"Thanks, Uncle Ray. This is a terrific gift."

Uncle Ray sat down next to him. "Once you start, your whiskers will grow out pretty regularly. Just rinse your face with warm water, and rub the gel on until it foams up. It doesn't take much. Give it a minute or two to soften

47

your whiskers and then shave using a downwards motion. It ought to be pretty smooth."

"This is the best gift, Uncle Ray. Thanks."

"And that's not all. I've got something else for you. It has to do with golf."

"Really?"

"Yes. Golf lessons to help you take your game to another level. You told me you wanted to beat your old man at golf someday, and I'm sure you will. But maybe you can make that happen sooner rather than later."

"That sounds great, Uncle Ray."

"Well, I've been thinking about golf lately. You know I used to play a lot myself when I was your age. We lived not far from a golf course and memberships were pretty cheap back then. So I played almost every day."

"You must have been pretty good."

"I loved the game. Your dad and I used to play golf with each other a lot. He was the better golfer. I probably should have taken some lessons. I taught myself how to play by reading books on golf and trying to do what they said. I couldn't afford lessons and anyway I didn't think I needed them. I know now that if someone had coached me in the basics, I'd have been a better golfer. So one of the local teaching pros is a friend of mine, and he's going to give you five lessons."

"Oh, man, that's fantastic! When?"

"You can start two weeks from this coming Saturday at five o'clock. Does that work for you?"

"Absolutely."

"He told me he'd look at your swing and give you some tips. The first lesson will be on the driver. Then one on short irons. Then one on putting and one on sand shots. The last one is a follow-up to check your progress."

"Are you going to take a lesson, too, Uncle Ray?"

"Not right now. I don't play much anymore. My work keeps me on the road a lot, and I'm not the player I used to be. But I was thinking I might take some lessons later and see if I can get my game back to where it used to be. Or better. Then we can play together."

"That would be awesome."

His uncle smiled. "I'm excited for you. These lessons will help you build the skills to play well. It's like I always say, actions have consequences. You'll be able to hit the shot you want if you execute the right swing."

"I can hardly wait."

"You know, there are a couple more areas that can help your game."

"What's that, Uncle Ray?"

"Well, one is your physical strength. I bet all that mowing you've been doing has helped you a lot."

"Yeah. I'm stronger than ever."

"In your upper body and your legs."

"Right."

"The pro can recommend some specific exercises to build the muscles and flexibility you need for golf. Does your school have a gym?"

"I think the high school has a weight room. But I'm only in the eighth grade."

"I tell you what. I belong to a gym not that far from your house. I could get you a membership there. It's not expensive. If I did, would you use it?"

"I think so."

"No, Chris. If I get you a membership, I'd want you to make a commitment. A one-hour workout, three times a week. Minimum."

"That sounds fine with me, Uncle Ray, but I've never worked out at a gym before."

"How about we go together one time first? You can decide whether you like it or not."

"That would be great."

"So. If you improve your skills, work on your physical strength, and get some good clubs, you ought to see a major improvement in your game. And there's one more thing. Actually, it's the thing that matters most when you're playing to win on the course."

"What's that?"

"It's the game between the ears."

Chris laughed. "The game between the ears? What's that?"

"Do you watch golf on TV? You know, PGA tournaments?"

"Not much. Sometimes with my dad."

"Check it out this weekend. Watching them play can give you insights about how the pros compete on the golf course. About the game between the ears. That's where the action is."

"I don't know what you're talking about, Uncle Ray."

"On any given Thursday, over a hundred pros are out there competing to win a championship. Chris, these guys have game. Every single one of them can pretty much do anything they want on the golf course. But the PGA only lets a couple hundred play on the tour. Which means there are ten times as many talented players out there who don't make it. And in any given tournament, one of the great players might fail to make the cut, and an unknown player might contend for the championship, which usually means a prize of about a million dollars."

"Wow. I don't think I'll ever be that good."

"Well, that remains to be seen. You don't have to be that good to make the golf team, play with your dad, and have a ton of fun. The point is, playing to win takes more than skill, physical strength and the best clubs. On the course, it comes down to whether you're strong as a person. Whether you're got the character and personal strengths to withstand adversity."

"What do you mean?"

"Say you make a bad shot. Say it goes into the trees. How does that make you feel? Do you get upset with yourself? If you let a mistake bother you, your emotions will affect your next shot. You'll probably make another bad shot."

"Yeah, I've done that."

"Or say it takes you three putts to get it into the hole. I bet you've done that before."

"Every time I play."

"Me, too. But when you're playing to win, it's virtually impossible to par a hole when you take three putts. I remember seeing a famous golfer take four putts."

"Really?"

"He was about forty feet from the hole, but he made a pretty good lag putt that ended up two feet from the hole. The thing is, he didn't take his time with that two-footer, and he pushed it three feet past. Then he was so upset he hurried his third putt and missed that one, too. Four putts to get it in the hole. A double bogey, which shook his confidence, and he played poorly the rest of the round. That four-putt was a game-changer for him and cost him half a million dollars that day."

"Wow."

"The problem wasn't his strength, or his skill, or his clubs. It was what was going on in his head, the mental aspect of the game—the game between the ears. Golf is a tough game, as you know, and being strong as a person in the face of adversity is what makes the difference when you're playing to win. It also makes the difference in life, when you're faced with challenges. The game between the ears has to do with an inner kind of strength. Personal strength. We talked about this before. It's that area of ability at the core of the onion, remember?"

"Yeah, I remember."

"There are dozens of personal strengths. Every sport requires a good mental game. For that matter, every aspect of life, no matter what, requires a good mental game—certain key personal strengths. You could be a doctor, a mechanic, a dancer, a teacher, a preacher, or a parent. No matter what you're doing in life, you need the strength to do the right thing and deal with adversity. A few of these strengths are especially important for playing competitive golf. When I tell you what they are, you'll be able to concentrate on them and be a better competitor."

"Okay."

"Here, take this pen and write down the name of the strength when I say it. Take notes if you want. The first is composure."

"Composure."

"I've seen great players crumble under pressure. A player might get excited or anxious or worried and it distracts him from hitting his normal shot. I remember watching Rory McIlroy, who was a young guy, only 22 when he won the U.S. Open in 2011. A few weeks before, at the Masters, he had a four-shot lead on the final day. All he had to do was keep playing his game and he would win his first major tournament. He was doing fine until he reached the final nine holes. He hit a bad shot, and he panicked. He lost control of his game, hit one bad shot after another, and ended up shooting an 80, which blew him out of contention."

"What could he have done differently?"

"Keeping your composure is all about channeling negative emotions aside. Not letting your emotions affect what you do next. You'll feel them. Everybody does. But if you can't walk away from them right away, if you can't calm down and concentrate on your shot, you're toast."

"Stay cool," Chris said.

"Right. Another key personal strength in golf is perseverance. Even top players make mistakes. You might take a risk and hit your ball into the water and make a double-bogey. If this happens to you, you can't say, 'Oh well, I can't win now.' You can't give up. You've got to keep trying, keep playing your best. A player who gives up won't try to do his best during the rest of the round. He can't win."

"What did you call that one again, Uncle Ray?"

"Perseverance. You keep on trying even though you have the urge to give up."

Chris wrote it down.

"The next strength is focus. At a golf tournament, there's a lot more going on than the game itself. There's the weather, the beauty of the course, and what the other players are doing. Anybody ever try to talk trash to you? Play with your mind?"

Chris laughed.

"You might think about a problem you're having in your personal life or something you want to do later that day. If you can't block out distractions and focus your attention 100% on the shot in front of you, you can't give it your best."

"Focus."

"Right. The next one is self-confidence. Golf is a challenging game. For me, it's the hardest game I've ever played. So many things can go wrong. Faced with a difficult shot, if you think you can't pull it off, you probably won't do what you have to do to. Confidence is about believing in your abilities. You earn confidence before you get on the course. It comes from making similar shots before, in practice and in competition, and giving yourself credit for that. It's easy to think that something hard can't be done. You have to believe you can do it."

"Another strength is thoroughness. In the world of work, we call this doing your due diligence. Taking care of business. In golf, they call it 'grinding it out.' To make sure you attempt the right kind of shot, you consider all the variables, such as changes in the wind, the slope of the ground, the wetness and texture of the sand or grass, the distance to the hole, the proximity of hazards, and the characteristics of the green."

"I usually focus mostly on my swing. I guess I need to learn more about this other stuff. It's a lot to think about."

"You're right. But the more you exercise these strengths, the easier they get. And oh yeah, I could have mentioned integrity. But that sort of goes without saying. Golf isn't a game for cheaters. The pros honor every rule. If you don't do that, you don't belong on the course."

"I'll write it down."

"So. Chris. Which one of these is your strong suit? Which one do you do most often, automatically?"

He studied the list: composure, perseverance, focus, self-confidence, thoroughness, integrity. He could see that all of them were important to playing golf. He thought maybe he should get stronger in every area.

"Integrity, I guess. I never cheat. I always play by the rules. That was the first thing Dad taught me. "Play it as it lies," he said.

"Your dad's right. If you get in the habit of cheating at golf, you'll start thinking you can cheat in other situations. In school. In your job. In relationships. Personal strengths are behavior patterns. Like habits. If you cheat, deep down you know you're a cheater. You won't like who you are. And eventually you'll get caught. Then people won't want to play golf with you. They won't want to work with you, because they won't trust you."

"I used to play golf with this guy who would lose his ball in the rough and then pretend to find it. He'd even lie about his score. I don't play golf with him anymore."

"I don't blame you. So which personal strength do you need to work on the most?"

Chris looked at the list again. "All of them."

"Pick the one you'd like to work on first. You can't work on all of them at the same time. That's spreading yourself too thin."

"Self-confidence, I guess. I never feel confident when I'm playing with somebody who's better than I am. I'm always worried I'll make a mistake."

"Good choice. You know, a lot of people don't give themselves enough credit. They discount their strong points, and that makes them doubt their ability. If you want to be more confident, you have to believe you're good at certain things. You need to get in the habit of saying to yourself, 'I can do this.'"

"What if I've never done something before? How do I know I can do it?"

"Because you've done other hard things. And you know other things that are related. If you're willing to give it your best shot, you can learn from the situation. Some of the stuff you try could work. You have to believe in your abilities."

"Get cocky."

"Yeah, just do it. You'll make mistakes sometimes, but you'll learn from them and get better at it. You see, a personal strength is more than a quality or an attribute. It's a behavior pattern. It's what you do habitually, how you act in situations. Getting stronger as a person is a lot like improving a skill, like hitting a golf ball. You want to get to the point that you do the right thing automatically. The only way to get to that point is to do it a lot."

"Learn by doing."

"Exactly! And after you apply what you know in your life, there's one more step."

"What's that?"

"Thinking about what you did. Ask yourself what happened, why, what were the consequences, and what could you do differently. This is how you learn from your experience."

"So I do it for real, then I think about it."

"That's right. And then you repeat that cycle. The more cycles of doing and then thinking about it, the stronger you get. It's like working out. Only instead of working on physical strength, you're working on personal strength."

"I get it."

"So guess what, guy? You're going to get some golf instruction. And you're going to be working out in two gyms! One for physical strength, and one for personal strength.

———————— ❖ ————————

"Being strong as a person in the face of adversity is what makes the difference when you're playing to win. It also makes the difference in life, when you're faced with challenges."

———————— ❖ ————————

The Golf Lesson

Standing behind his uncle's car in the parking lot, Chris put on his golf shoes. His uncle waved in the direction of the clubhouse. Chris looked up to see a man in a red polo shirt and khaki slacks waving back.

As they approached the clubhouse, the man came to meet them. "Hi, I'm Emilio Sanchez." He smiled and shook Chris's hand. He looked like a guy who worked out a lot. "I'm a teaching pro at the country club on the other side of town."

"Hi, Emilio," said Uncle Ray. "Thanks for coming over."

"My pleasure. So, Chris. You want to improve your game."

"Yes." He was excited. He'd never had a lesson before, and he wasn't sure what would happen.

"I'll be with you for an hour today. What do you want to work on first?"

"I'd like to be longer off the tee. If that's possible."

"Longer off the tee. And keep it in the fairway, right? We can do that. Why don't we go over to the practice range."

They walked over to a long, elevated area that opened to a vast green field. Several golfers were hitting balls. Emilio took them to a position at the far end of the range. Two buckets of white balls were waiting for them.

"Okay, Chris. Why don't you get out your favorite club and warm up by hitting a few balls easy."

Chris got out his 7-iron, took a few practice swings, and then hit a few balls.

"I think I'm ready," he said.

"All right. Now get your driver and let's see you hit a few."

Chris was nervous. His uncle had never seen him play, and he didn't want to make a fool of himself. To calm down, he imagined that he was just out playing with friends. He set one of the balls on a tee and stood over it. *Just nice and smooth,* he said to himself. He took what he thought was his normal swing. When he connected with the ball and saw it sailing straight ahead, he breathed a sigh of relief.

"Good," said Emilio. "I'll just stand behind you while you hit a few more."

Chris teed up another ball and took his best swing. This one curved to the left. After hitting half a dozen balls, Emilio said, "Okay, Chris, that's great. Let's take a break and talk about what you're doing here."

"Okay."

"First of all, I like your grip. It's perfect. I wouldn't change a thing there. Everything begins with the grip and you're solid. Also, I like the way you address the ball. You go through the same routine each time. That's important. Your posture is good and you're relaxed. You've got the ball a little forward, which is just right. Good fundamentals, Chris."

"Thanks."

"I think I see a couple things that will make a big difference for you. I'd like you to try something. Are you open to that?"

"Sure."

"The first thing is the plane of your swing. It's quite a bit flatter than it should be. Do you know what I mean?"

"No."

"Here, let me show you. Stand in front of the ball as if you're going to hit another drive. Then bring the club back and hold it at the top of your swing."

When Chris did that, the pro held his hands in place. "Very good, Chris. It feels natural, doesn't it?"

Emilio took a club from Chris's bag and demonstrated a backswing. "This is what I see." He repeated the motion a couple more times. "Now I'm going to show you what is considered an ideal backswing." He demonstrated it, sweeping the club back several times. "Do you see the difference? Do you see that your arc happens at a much lower angle?"

"Yes."

"You see, a flat swing tends to produce a hook. With a flat swing, the only way to keep it in the fairway is to compensate, but it's hard to control. You never know how much hook you're going to get. And you sacrifice distance. Quite a bit of distance. This might feel a little weird to you, Chris, but now I'm going to move your hands to where they should be at the top of your swing."

"Okay."

The pro gently moved his hands to a position higher and further out from his body. He also repositioned the club. "Right there. How does that feel?"

"Terrible. It feels totally wrong."

"I'm not surprised. It feels strange to you because it's different. Now Chris, I want you to address the ball, and I want you to slowly begin your backswing while I guide your hands to this position. Okay?"

"Okay."

Emilio helped him do this about ten times. "Now let's tee up a ball, and you bring the club back just that way and then follow through. Hit the shot."

Chris wiped sweat from his eyes. He brought the club back slowly. "Like this?" he said.

"You're dropping down a little." He repositioned his hands. "Try it again."

"This is hard," said Chris. He wasn't sure this change was going to work for him. It felt all wrong. But he tried hard to do what the pro said.

"That's it," said Emilio. "Now do it again, and follow through with a hit."

When Chris took his swing, he was off balance and hit the top of the ball, sending it rocketing into the ground. The pro encouraged him to try it again, but the next few swings weren't much better.

Chris felt discouraged. "Mr. Sanchez, I don't know if I can do this."

Emilio put a hand on his shoulder and said, "Chris, actually, you're doing better than you think. Your position at the top of the swing is crucial, but it's only one part of your swing. You have to make it a part of everything else. This will take some practice. Now I have two tips that could make it easier for you. I'd like you to try them. You game?"

"Okay. I'll try whatever you say."

"Great. First I want you to slow your backswing down a little bit. You're rushing it a little, maybe because you're trying to put your strength into it. I think that's why you bring your swing tight into your body. If you'll relax and slow it down a little, you'll be able to control your swing better. Clubhead speed doesn't come from bringing the club back fast. It comes from whipping the club in the downswing. Make sense?"

"I think so."

"Just think, nice and easy as you go back to this position right here."

Chris tried it.

"Even a little slower, Chris."

"Okay."

"Try that a few times without a ball. Nice and easy."

Chris concentrated on bringing the club back slowly. That felt awkward, too. Everything felt wrong.

"That's better," said Emilio. He teed up a ball. He laid a club behind the ball, the shaft pointing straight back from the ball. I want you to bring your clubhead back over the shaft nice and easy. When your hands are in the correct position, whip the clubhead down though the ball."

Chris tried his best to do that. He heard the click when he connected, but he didn't feel a thing. He looked up to see the ball sailing far in the distance.

"Wow."

"Wow," said Uncle Ray.

"Wow," said the pro. "You did it, Chris. You did it perfectly. How did it feel?"

"It felt wonderful. I did what you said, but I don't know if I can do it again."

"Well, my friend, that's what we're going to do with the rest of our hour. You're going to hit the rest of these balls. And while you do that, I'll try to keep you in the groove."

And that's what they did. Chris hit over a hundred balls while Emilio said, "nice and easy" and made little corrections. Most of the balls were sailing straight, and farther than he'd been able to hit them before.

"How far do you think that one went?"

"I'd say more than 200 yards. In the air."

"Wow."

"Pretty good, Chris. Does it feel comfortable yet?"

"It still feels a little weird. I wouldn't say comfortable."

"That's about right. Comfortable won't come until you've hit a couple thousand balls."

"Really?"

"Yes. That's my assignment for you before our next lesson. Hit forty buckets of balls with your driver. Will you do that?"

"He will," said Uncle Ray. "He comes to the course almost every day. I'll come with him and watch his swing."

"Perfect," said Emilio.

Back in the clubhouse, Chris and his uncle sat at a table drinking iced tea. "I feel like a burger," said Uncle Ray. "How about you?"

"That sounds great."

"And fries."

"Yeah."

"Emilio's a good guy. I think I'll take a few lessons from him myself."

"That would be great. We should play together sometime."

"Okay, but I'll need to work on my game first. If we're going to have some fun out there, that is."

"I need more lessons, too. That was an awesome lesson."

"You did great."

"It's funny. That may be the right way to hit the ball, but it feels so wrong."

"You want to know why?"

"Yeah, why?"

"You remember I was telling you that stuff about how the decision-making part of your brain needs to wire itself up? And to do that, you have to exercise it?"

"I remember."

"Well golf's the same way. Only swinging a golf club involves a different part of your brain. And you've already got it wired for golf. You've been playing golf for a few years now—plenty long enough to connect the brain cells. You're wired. But some of your wiring is wrong for a great golf swing. You taught yourself some bad habits. I did the same thing when I was young."

"You did?"

"So hitting a drive the old way, the wrong way, feels natural and comfortable. Hitting it the right way doesn't. It's because you have to rewire the golf part of your brain. And that will take a lot of practice. It's the repetitions that make the brain cells connect to each other. At first, that will mean a lot of not giving up when your swing doesn't feel right and the shots don't go where they're supposed to. If you practice what he told you enough, your brain will rewire itself, and then your new swing will feel comfortable. You gotta do the reps. That's how it works in golf, and that's how it works with everything you do in life. Even when you're trying to get stronger as a person."

"I see."

"As your coach, I'm going to make sure you get your swings in."

"I will, Uncle Ray."

"Actually, you could be your own coach. All you have to do is stay calm when you hit a bad shot. Ask yourself what you did and see how that affected the shot. Then focus on how you're going to hit your next shot. If you can do that, you can be your own coach."

"Why and what if questions, right?"

"That's right, guy. Here come our burgers."

───────── ❖ ─────────

– REFLECTION –
Take ACTION, then ask yourself
"The Five Magic Questions"

What happened?
Why did it happen that way?
What were the consequences?
What should I do differently in the
future?
What are my next steps?

───────── ❖ ─────────

"You gotta do the reps."

ACTION – REFLECTION
ACTION – REFLECTION
ACTION – REFLECTION
ACTION – REFLECTION
ACTION – REFLECTION
ACTION – REFLECTION
ACTION – REFLECTION

───────── ❖ ─────────

The Golf Lesson

Tempers Flare

It was the fall of Chris's freshman year, and one day when he didn't arrive home on time after school, Sherry, his mom, began to worry. An hour later, Chris still wasn't home and hadn't called. She called him, but he didn't answer, so she left a message. Another hour passed, and it was time to start dinner. But first she called Uncle Ray. He said he hadn't seen him. When scary scenarios started rushing through her mind, she called her husband, Roger, who was on his way home. "If he's not back by the time I get there, I'll start calling around," he said.

Ten minutes later, the front door opened and Chris walked in.

"Chris, where have you been?"

"Nowhere, Mom," he said as he headed for his room.

"Wait a minute, son. I want to talk to you." She followed him down the hall, but Chris had closed the bedroom door behind him.

She called through the door: "What's going on? I've been worried sick."

"It's nothing, mom."

"What do you mean, nothing! I had no idea where you were. Even your uncle didn't know where you were. I was afraid something might have happened to you."

A loud groan came through the door. "You called Uncle Ray? What the hell, Mom? Are you spying on me? Can't I have a life without you watching every move I make?"

"Please come out. You can tell me about it while I make dinner."

"Can't I have a little privacy around here? I don't want any dinner! Leave me alone!"

The irritation in her son's voice was like a physical blow. *Who is this child? Where is my little boy?*

Sherry wasn't sure how to handle this situation. She knew something was wrong. Maybe Chris was in trouble, but she couldn't imagine what it could be. She felt she ought to say something, but she was at a loss for words. Afraid of making the situation worse, she returned to the kitchen. As she stood at the sink, tears ran down her cheeks.

When Roger came home, he found her in the kitchen. After she told him what had happened, he strode down the hall and banged on Chris's door. "Open the door."

"Leave me alone, Dad."

"I said open the door!" His voice echoed in the hallway. Chris unlocked the door, and his father rushed in.

"What's going on, son? Why were you so late getting home? Where were you? What do you think gives you the right to talk to your mother that way?"

"Dad, it's no big deal."

"Answer me!"

"Nothing happened. It's nothing."

"What do you mean, nothing? You were rude to your mother! I want you to go apologize to her and tell us what's going on."

"All right, all right!" As he stormed out of the room, he pushed his father aside. Roger lost his balance, knocked down a lamp, and found himself sitting on the floor. Before he could do anything about it, his son had left the house. He chased after him, but by the time he reached the street, Chris was nowhere in sight.

When Chris got to Uncle Ray's house, he found his uncle sitting on the porch. He nodded as Chris climbed the stairs. "Hey. What's up?"

"I had a big argument with my parents."

"Yeah, I heard. Your dad just called. I'd like to call him back and tell him you're with me and you're okay. You don't have to talk to him, and you can stay here as long as you want. Okay?"

"Okay."

After his uncle put his phone back in his pocket, he smiled at Chris. "Everything's okay," he said.

Chris looked out at the street, and the two of them sat in silence as the sky darkened.

"Uncle Ray?"

"What?"

"Why can't my mom and dad just let me have a life?"

"Tell me about it. What happened?"

"After school I went to the golf course to look at new grips for my clubs. This guy came in and wanted a caddy so I went out with him. Afterward, I came straight home. Mom is all over me like I've done something wrong. It drives me crazy. Then Dad comes home and gets in my face. That's when I took off."

"Why do you think your mom was acting that way?"

"How should I know? I have a right to my life. I'm a good kid. I don't deserve to be treated like that."

"Like how?"

"Watching every move I make. Telling me what to do. I have absolutely no privacy."

"Chris, try to imagine that you're the mother and your son didn't come home from school. Why do you think she acted that way?"

Chris thought about it. "I guess she got worried."

"Why would your mother worry?"

"I don't know. I never get in trouble. Maybe she just worries a lot."

"Didn't she know where you were?"

"I don't know. If I'm not at home I'm either at school or at the golf course. I figured she knew. I guess I could have called her."

"Do you think that would have kept her from worrying?

"I guess so."

"So you and your dad had it out?"

"Yeah, it was weird."

"What happened?"

"He banged on my door and shouted at me like I was stupid or something."

"Sounds like he was pretty mad. What was he mad about?"

"He said I was rude to Mom."

"Were you?"

"No. But she was on my case and wouldn't leave me alone."

They sat silently for a while as the evening darkened.

Then Uncle Ray said, "It sounds like cooler heads did not prevail. Sounds like everyone got upset and you took off."

"Yeah, that's what happened all right."

"So your parents blew their cool. But you did, too. Do you know why?"

"Uncle Ray, do we have to keep talking about this?"

"I promised you I'd be your coach, remember? Get you to think about why and what if?"

"Yeah."

"Okay, let's get to the point. These flare-ups don't happen very often, do they?"

"No."

"So when they do, you want to figure out why it happened, so you can handle it better next time, right?"

"I guess so."

"So. Why did you blow your cool?"

"Because my parents were all over me and I didn't do anything wrong. I couldn't stand it."

"You got angry."

"Uncle Ray, you don't have to live there. You don't know what it's like."

"You're right. And you know what? If I were your age and in that situation I probably would have reacted the same way. And the result would probably have been the same. So what were the consequences, Chris?"

"Well, I'm here. With you."

"Right. And how about your parents? Everything fine there?"

"No, I guess not."

"That's right. Nobody's perfect, Chris. Not you, and not your parents. Your mom probably expected you to come home at the usual time and when you didn't, she started worrying. She got emotional and so you got emotional. This is what imperfect people do. But it causes hurt feelings. It damages relationships. Your parents may wonder if they can trust you."

"Trust me? For what?"

"For starters, how about trusting you to be home on time or to let them know where you are? Chris, you're about to find out that whether your parents trust you is more important than you thought."

"What do you mean?"

"When is your curfew?"

"Curfew?"

"When are you required to be at home at night?"

"I'm supposed to be home for supper."

"And what if your friends want to do something in the evening? When do you have to be back home?"

"By ten."

"But someday your friends may want to stay out later. You'd want your parents to allow it, right?"

"Sure."

"What would make them let you do it?"

"If it's like to a movie or something safe, they should go along with it."

"That's reasonable, but what it comes down to is whether they trust you. If they trust you, they'll let you do it. If they don't, they won't. They want to be sure you're safe and you'll stay out of trouble. They need to trust that you'll use good judgment."

"They should trust me. I'm a good kid."

"Yes, you are. But losing your temper like you did earlier doesn't count in your favor. It makes them wonder. Later, when you get your driver's license, if they don't trust you to make good choices they won't give you the keys to the car. People get killed in cars all the time. They need to trust that you'll come home safe."

After a long silence, Chris said, "What should I do now?"

"What would make them start trusting you again?"

"I don't know, I guess I overreacted. Maybe I should apologize."

"I think your parents overreacted, too. But you know what? You're right. Apologizing is a very adult thing to do. It's what a man would do. Just take responsibility for what happened and tell them you're sorry. Tell them that in the future you'll keep them in the loop and consider their feelings."

"You think that will work?"

"It's a great start. Then you can just keep on doing the things that will cause them to trust you more."

"Like calling to let them know where I am."

"Right."

"You know, it's amazing to me that all this happened. It's crazy."

Uncle Ray nodded. "You're right. Nothing logical about it. Hey, while we're on the subject, why do you suppose you acted that way? You know, hot-heated instead of calm and collected?"

"I don't know. I was just mad all of a sudden."

"Like I've been telling you, the decision-making part of your brain is still under construction. It's hard to be logical when your brain is still programming itself for logic. It's a whole lot easier to just react emotionally."

"So what I am supposed to do?"

"Well, Aristotle said that to get good at something, you have to do it a lot. So if you want to become a more logical person, you have to make yourself think logically. It's like golf. To get a good putting stroke, you have to hit a lot of putts, the right way."

"But if I get mad, how do I stay calm?"

"Good point. If keeping cool were easy, everybody'd do it. But I have a few suggestions."

"What?"

"First, the next time you get steamed, it doesn't matter why, it could be something that happens at school. Or maybe you miss a shot on the golf course. Or maybe your mom does something that gets on your nerves. The next time you feel mad, try this. Take three slow, deep breaths, and ask yourself this question – 'What's the most effective thing I can do right now?' Try that."

"Do you really think that'll work?"

"If you actually do it, yes, I think it will. For one thing, it'll keep you from reacting immediately. It'll give you a few seconds to calm down. And it'll cause you to use the smart part of your brain, the part that needs exercise right now. Maybe you'll think of something that will give you a good result. What happened tonight certainly wasn't a good result."

"Right."

"The second thing you can do is to listen."

"Listen? Listen to what?"

"Remember the people skills ring of the onion?"

"Yeah."

"Listening is a people skill. I'm not just talking about physically hearing what someone says. I mean making sure you understand what they're trying to say. One reason everything flared up today was because neither you nor your parents did much listening."

"I heard what they said, all right."

"But you didn't get what they meant, what they were trying to tell you. When you listen effectively you realize that somebody's trying to tell you something, even though they may not be communicating very well."

"So what was I supposed to do?"

"You ask yourself, what are they trying to say? When you think you know, check it out. See if you understood it right."

"I don't get it."

"What you do is tell the other person what you think they meant, in your own words. I'll give you an example. Remember what your mom was saying outside your room? You could have said, 'Mom, it sounds like you're upset because you didn't know where I was.' If you had said that, what do you think would have happened?"

"I guess she would have agreed with me. But Uncle Ray, I can't imagine doing that. I was mad."

"That's right. It's a different way of reacting to someone. I didn't say this was easy. I said it's effective. But if you knew then what you know now, and if you could have forced yourself to do it, the conversation would have been much different. What happened next would have been a lot different."

"That's a big if, Uncle Ray."

"I know. It isn't easy when your habitual way of reacting is to do something else. It's not easy to hit a golf ball out of a sand trap, either. You have to know what to do, and then practice it. So, do you know what to do?"

"Instead of popping off, I ask myself what's the most effective thing, and I calm down. Then I focus on what Mom or Dad is trying to say. I tell them what I think it is. Is that all there is to it?"

"Pretty much. Don't worry if you forget to do it or if it doesn't work well the first few times. Don't give up. You wouldn't give up on your sand shot, so don't give up on communicating with your folks."

"Okay."

"Are you hungry?"

"Yeah."

"I bet your mom made a great dinner. I'll take you home now, and you can take care of business."

"The next time you feel mad, try this. Take three slow, deep breaths, and ask yourself this question – 'What's the most effective thing I can do right now?'"

"Whatever we learn to do, we learn by actually doing it: men come to be builders, for instance, by building, and harp players by playing the harp. In the same way, by doing just acts, we come to be just; by doing self-controlled acts, we come to be self-controlled; and by doing brave acts, we become brave."
- Aristotle, Greek philosopher (B.C. 384-322)

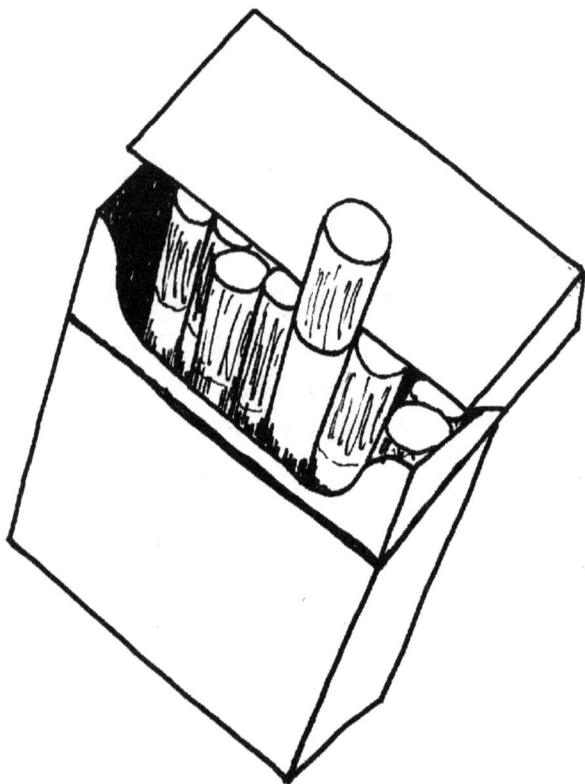

One of the Guys

One day when Chris was fifteen, he and Uncle Ray sat on folding chairs in front of his uncle's open garage door, cleaning and oiling tools.

"You don't smoke, do you, Uncle Ray?"

"No, I don't. I've never had one puff of a cigarette. Not once. I did smoke a pipe for a while. And I've puffed a few cigars." He was quiet for a moment. Then he said, "And I got high on marijuana once."

"What was that like?"

"It was pretty weird. It screwed up my perception and made it hard to think straight. I wasn't my usual self the next day. Later I found out that using it regularly can damage your brain. Permanently. So I never did it again. Why do you ask?"

"Some of the guys at school offered me a cigarette."

"Did you try it?"

"I said no thanks."

"Good for you. Why did you decide not to try it?"

"I didn't want to get into the habit. I hear it's easy to get hooked."

"And hard to quit," said Uncle Ray. "I know people who've tried to quit off and on for years and always go back."

"I'm working on flexibility and strength fitness, so smoking doesn't make sense to me. My friends who are athletes don't smoke, either."

"And it causes lung cancer and increases your chance for heart disease."

"The guy who offered me the cigarette, I can smell smoke on his clothes. It's disgusting."

"So why do you think kids do it?"

"I guess they think it's cool and they don't think about getting hooked. Maybe they see adults smoking and figure it'll make them look grown up."

"So you weren't really tempted?"

"I was a little curious. But I knew my parents would go ballistic if they caught me smoking. And I knew you wouldn't like it."

"True. I once had a professor in college who smoked. She'd sometimes have a coughing fit during a lecture, that dry smoker's hack. I heard recently that they had to take one of her lungs and now she has to have chemo."

"That's scary."

"Another thing. Smoking is expensive. If you smoke a pack a day, it adds up to over a thousand dollars a year. Some smokers go through two packs a day. That would run about three thousand dollars a year."

"That's more than my golf clubs cost!"

"Right. I say, if you're going to get addicted to something, get addicted to exercise. Get addicted to travel. Get addicted to learning. A lot of people do. Get addicted to something that builds you up, not tears you down."

"It's stupid to think cigarettes make you seem grown up," said Chris. "I guess that's why kids drink, too."

"Have you ever had a drink?"

"I drank some beer once."

"Did you like it?"

"It was okay. But not something I'd want to do all the time."

"So why do you think so many kids want to drink?"

"They want to have a good time."

"And like you said, it's another way to try to act grown up without actually being grown up. But getting drunk isn't a good way to have fun. It's risky business."

"It's illegal until you're twenty-one."

"That's right, though in some states the legal age is less. The problem is that having one drink can get you in the mood for another. That's when it starts to affect your judgment. Having several drinks can make you think that doing something crazy is the perfect thing to do."

"Because I might forget to think about what could happen."

"It's partly because of the alcohol and partly because kids that age have a hard time using the decision-making part of their brain. If they get a buzz on, they might decide to do something exciting like getting in a car and bombing around town. If they're caught, they'll be charged with DUI. There could be big fines. They could lose their licenses. And the insurance company could triple or quadruple the price for car insurance. Worse things could happen."

"Like a car accident."

"Exactly. Alcohol not only impairs your judgment, it slows your reactions. It makes it easy to lose control or run into another car. People could die, Chris. Innocent people."

They were silent for a moment, and then Chris said softly, "One of my dad's friends is an alcoholic. Dad says he's mean when he drinks."

"It's an addictive substance. It can be hard on relationships. And it can be hard on the body. Your body sees alcohol as a poison and has to work hard to get rid of it."

"Yeah, I know."

"To me, the worst thing about a teenager drinking alcohol is what it can do to your brain. And I'm not talking about killing off a few hundred brain cells."

"What do you mean?"

"It's like when doctors warn mothers not to smoke or drink during pregnancy. The danger is that the substance will go from the mother's body to the baby's body during a sensitive growth period. If that happens, the alcohol could disrupt normal development and cause a defect in the baby's body or brain."

"Yeah, Mom told me about that."

"Most people don't know that for teenagers, the front part of their brain is in a similar sensitive growth period, what you and I have talked about before. The danger is the same, that it could disrupt normal development, cause a defect in the brain, in the part of the brain that's for higher-level thinking. Permanent brain damage."

"I never thought about that. Uncle Ray, alcohol isn't a big deal for me like it is for some of my friends. I stay away from it."

"I know you do. But let me ask you this. What if your friends want to do something you know is risky? Would you go along, take a chance, to be one of the guys? If you didn't, they might think you're some kind of prude or party pooper."

"My friends aren't like that."

"You must be hanging out with the right friends. But someone offered you a cigarette, right? Someday you may find yourself in a group that gets a crazy idea to do something they shouldn't. What will you do then?"

"Uncle Ray, I know people do stupid things sometimes. That's not me. I'd just say, 'You guys go ahead. I have something else I have to do.'"

"And if they try to talk you into it? If they kid you or say mean things to you?"

"Then they're not my friends."

"You got that right. But peer pressure can be tough for a teenager. Kids want to be liked. They want other kids to think they're cool. They might want to be popular so much that they'd go along with whatever the cool crowd is doing. Dress a certain way. Act a certain way. Do what they do, even if it's stupid. Or illegal. Or even dangerous. And then later, when things go bad, they wonder what they were thinking about."

"Maybe they weren't thinking. Just having fun."

"Exactly. But Chris, it can be hard when your friends keep pressuring you to do something you don't want to do. So I want to give you something that might help. An out."

"An out? What do you mean?"

"I mean you should feel free to use your parents, or even me as an excuse. All you have to do is say something like, 'This sounds like fun, but I've got two strikes against me right now and if my dad got wind of this it would be really, really bad for me. You all have fun, but count me out on this one.' It's an escape out."

"I see. That might work."

"Use it if you have to. It's better than doing something you'll regret for the rest of your life."

❖

"Peer pressure can be tough for a teenager. Kids want to be liked. They want other kids to think they're cool. They might want to be popular so much that they'd go along with whatever the cool crowd is doing. Dress a certain way. Act a certain way. Do what they do, even if it's stupid. Or illegal. Or even dangerous. And then later, when things go bad, they wonder what they were thinking about."

❖

"The problem is that having one drink can get you in the mood for another. That's when it starts to affect your thinking. Having several drinks can make you think that doing something crazy is the perfect thing to do."

❖

One of the Guys

Giving Back

Chris had just finished his sophomore year, and he was sitting alone at a table in a coffee shop in downtown Little Rock, where he and his uncle often came for breakfast. He spread some strawberry cream cheese on his bagel and took a bite. He was thinking that he hadn't seen his uncle in three weeks when he saw him enter the café. He got up and gave him a hug.

"Good to see you," said Uncle Ray. "My visit took longer than it was supposed to."

"What were you doing, Uncle Ray?"

"My company is coming out with something new, and they wanted to test it with real people. I needed to be there to see their reactions first hand and figure out what changes to make. But look at you, man. You're putting on some serious muscle."

"I've been working out. That's a great gym, Uncle Ray."

"How's the golf? Have you beaten your dad yet?"

"You know, Uncle Ray, beating my dad isn't a big deal for me. I just want to be a scratch golfer."

"That's quite a goal."

"You know I've been practicing, hitting balls on the driving range. I help out there and they let me hit for free. I've been hitting a ton of balls. Plus there's a guy there who sometimes gives me pointers."

"You keep this up and you'll be the captain of the golf team."

"I don't know about that."

"Hey listen. I'm sorry about Alexander."

"Yeah, he was in pretty bad shape. It was time. But I think about him a lot."

"Of course you do. He was a best friend your whole life."

"Yeah."

Uncle Ray waved at the waitress. "I'll have what he's having," he said.

Chris looked around the room. A guy in a suit was eating something that looked like a burrito. At another table, four kids about his age were laughing. He and his uncle were silent for several minutes while they sipped coffee.

"Uncle Ray?"

"What?"

"What happens to dogs when they die?"

"You mean, does the dog's soul go to heaven?"

"I guess."

"To be honest, I don't know for sure."

"Do you go to church, Uncle Ray?"

"Yes. Not every week, but I like going with your grandma and grandpa. How about you?"

"Mom and Dad take us most Sundays. But to tell you the truth, I'm not sure that church is for me. It's boring. Most of the time I can't wait for it to be over."

"Well, you know you don't always have to do what your parents do."

"I know."

"You can follow any faith you want. Have you given that any thought?"

"Not much. But lately I've been wondering."

"That maybe you should?"

"I asked Mom about it and she said it's my choice. Whatever church I go to, or whether I go at all, it's my choice."

"I'd say she's right."

"But there are so many religions. It's confusing."

"You can check some of them out, see if they have a teen group. You're growing up and it's a good idea to give serious thought to life's big questions. Like, who am I? Why am I here? Where did all this come from? What happens to me when I die?"

"Where did you find your answers, Uncle Ray?"

"You know, your grandparents go to church almost every Sunday. I grew up with that, and it's always been a positive in my life. A lot of the people there were kind to me, helped me when I was a kid. Then there was a time after I left the Army that I got curious about other religions."

"What did you do?"

"I started reading, looking for answers. I wanted to know more about the world and the universe, where it all came from. One thing I found out is that most of what's going on here on Earth and in the universe is still a mystery. For example, scientists aren't really sure what gravity is. And after hundreds of years of research, they still don't know what light is. There are theories, but the theories keep changing. So they're always inquiring into things. They embrace theories when the evidence makes sense, even when they aren't totally sure. They accept the theories on faith. You know what I mean by faith?"

"You mean they believe, even though they don't have absolute proof?"

"Right. They take it on faith, until better evidence comes along. And that's what I do, I guess. I try to find out what makes sense, then I say, 'This is what I believe.' When it comes to religion, I take a lot of things on faith. I guess I've come full circle. I still like that old church and the people in it. They're almost like family. Most of all, I believe that if I live a good life and treat people right, I'll be fine. My faith plays a big part in that."

Chris took another sip of his coffee.

Uncle Ray kept talking. "I was visiting with a young woman last week. She was in her mid-twenties. She had a miserable childhood. Count your blessings, Chris. Not everyone has nice parents. I won't go into it. It's a tragic story. Anyway, the bottom line is, she's fine today. She told me that what got her through was the time she spent with her grandparents. And going to church. The people there helped her. It was a good place for her to retreat to. It gave her hope."

"I'm glad it worked for her, but that doesn't mean it'll work for me."

"Spirituality is a personal thing. It's amazing how many paths there are, and they're all different. Whatever you decide has to work for you. So you see, only you can make that choice."

"I know."

"But to get your answers, you have to ask the questions. Until you resolve these questions for yourself, it'll be like being adrift on the ocean. You need to find your solid ground. Answer those big questions for yourself."

Chris gazed out the window.

"Back to your original question, I know some people who would say Alexander has a soul and it's in heaven now. Others would say no, only humans have souls. There are even people who believe there's no such thing as a soul. It's a matter of faith, what you choose to believe. The bottom line is, your little buddy is gone, and you miss him. It's hard. The way to get through it is to go ahead and feel sad. Over time you'll get used to his absence, and you'll remember the good things and they'll make you smile. It's what happens when we lose someone we care about. Someday you might even get a new dog."

"I don't think so."

Uncle Ray took a bite from his bagel and sipped his coffee. "Hey, tomorrow is my day for Habitat for Humanity. You want to come along?"

"What's that?"

"It's community service. I spend a morning every week with a crew that builds homes for needy families. I like doing it. I get to use my skills and it helps keep me in shape. I'd love for you to come with me once."

"Really?"

"We could sure use the help, and it would be a good experience for you. You've got some carpentry skills, and you might learn something new. School's out. Why don't you put on your

Mr. Curiosity hat? Find out what's going on in the world."

"Okay. Count me in."

The worksite was in a new development north of Little Rock. Chris could see that several homes were in varying stages of completion.

The crew supervisor was a guy named Rick. At first he asked Chris to bring lumber and fetch hardware, then whatever jobs needed doing. Uncle Ray and a guy named Eltoro were on the other end of the site putting up studs. Eltoro was a student at the Bowen School of Law.

At one point Rick asked, "Do you know how to operate this saw?"

"No. Can you show me?"

Rick showed him the basics and emphasized some points of safety. He showed Chris how to measure for a cut. "Measure twice, cut once," he said. "Always put your blade on the line, not next to it. And use these ear muffs. That saw's pretty loud. Don't go too fast. Respect the saw. You don't want this to happen to you." He held up his left hand. Chris saw that a finger was missing.

Later, Chris and his uncle took a water break as they sat on the edge of the foundation. It wasn't a particularly hot day, but they had worked up a sweat.

"So what do you think? Is this a good way to spend a morning?"

"Rick taught me how to use the saw, and now I'm the saw guy. They tell me what they want, and I measure it and cut it."

"Fantastic."

"I learned something new. And I got a workout."

"You might be able to use some of what you learned this summer. You want me to contact my construction buddy?"

"Do you think I could talk to him? Find out what I'd be doing?"

"Sure. I'll let you know when he starts hiring."

"I could use the money."

"Those clubs must have emptied your savings account."

"They did."

"So, you think you'd like to help out on the site here again? Maybe you'll pick up some more skills."

"Maybe."

"You know the real reason I do this, Chris?"

"No, why?"

"You've heard the phrase, 'give back'? Well, you can't always give back to the people who helped you out when you needed it. You give back to the world. There are times when people need a helping hand. I like Habitat for Humanity because it lets me do what I do best, and people are going to be helped in a big way. This house is for a single mother who has three kids. Without this, she couldn't afford to own a home. It will make a big difference for that family."

"Do you know her?"

"No, I haven't met her. They selected her because she's trying, and she's put in a ton of hours helping build homes for other families."

"So now it's her turn."

"Yes. So you see why I feel good about this program. I'm involved in something larger than myself. It makes me feel I'm the kind of guy who helps people." He smiled. "And so are you, partner. Today you stepped up. You gave back."

Chris smiled back. "I guess I did. Uncle Ray, have you ever had to struggle?"

"Of course. Everyone struggles one time or another. Life has a way of dishing up surprises. When my wife died of cancer, it was about as bad as things get."

"I remember."

"I was laid off once, a long time ago. The economy went bad, and my company eliminated my job. It was hard to find a new one. I had to work in a convenience store for a while."

"I didn't know about that."

"It turned out okay. I learned about business from the customer's perspective, you know, about good service and how to deal with people. In the long run I ended up working for a big company, which allowed me to be creative and make more money. But when life dished up lemons, I had to make lemonade. I had to make something happen. Chris, sooner or later we all need help. So when we contribute like this, it's a way to give back. And we're stronger for it. Does this make sense?"

"I think so."

"Community service would be one more thing on your full plate."

"Yeah, I know."

"If not Habitat for Humanity, then something else. Maybe a worthy cause some of your friends are involved in. Or you could organize something new, a way of helping people that doesn't exist yet, something you care about."

Chris was quiet.

"I don't want to push you. If you feel like you want to contribute, you will. When you want. How you want. You know I'd love to have you out here with me, but it doesn't matter."

"We'll see."

"That's fine. If something does turn you on, let me know about it, okay?"

"Sure."

———————— ❖ ————————

"Spirituality is a personal thing. It's amazing how many paths there are, and they're all different. Whatever you decide has to work for you. So you see, only you can make that choice."

———————— ❖ ————————

"I'm involved in something larger than myself. It makes me feel like I'm the kind of guy who helps people."

———————— ❖ ————————

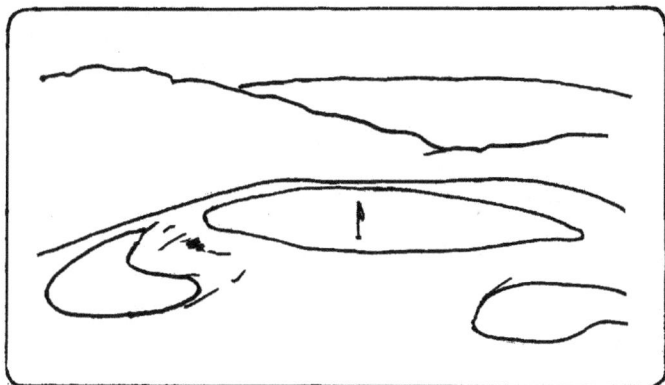

You Da Man

The summer between Chris's junior and senior year, he and Uncle Ray were on the golf course. Chris was golfing with his friend, Hideki, and Uncle Ray was driving the cart. They were on the eighth tee, a par three hole. The green, 185 yards away, was elevated with deep traps on both sides.

"Actually, the green has two levels," said Chris. "See how it rises in the back?"

"Looks like a monster," Hideki said.

"But if I give it a full swing and get it to land beyond the hole, the grade should bring the ball back some. And I avoid the traps."

"Can you do that?"

"I'm going to try."

Chris took an easy practice swing. Then he stepped up to the ball. Without hesitation, he brought the club back and whipped it through the shot.

The ball sailed high, then curved slightly toward the green. It landed softly on the back part of the green. And just as Chris predicted, the ball began to roll back toward the hole. By the time it stopped, it was only fifteen or twenty feet from the hole.

"Nice," said Uncle Ray.

"Birdie putt coming up," said Chris with a smile.

After Chris's friend hit, they got in the cart and headed for the hole. Uncle Ray said, "I have to tell you, you're way out of my league now."

"I've worked hard at it. And now the game is more fun than ever. Did I tell you I got a scholarship offer? I played with the Arkansas coach last week, and he says he wants me on the team."

"That's fabulous. And you're only a rising senior."

"They're recruiting juniors, too."

"You're playing well today. One under par, so far."

"If this putt isn't tricky, maybe it will be two under," Chris said with a confident smile.

When they reached the hole, they saw that Hideki's ball was in the left sand trap. He was able to blast it onto the green, but it ran to the back edge. It would be a long putt. While his friend prepared to putt, Chris studied the green. When it was his turn, he stood over the ball. He looked relaxed. He stroked it, and the ball curved towards the hole. Then it straightened and dropped into the cup.

"That's what I'm talking about," he said. "Birdie!"

In the car on the way back from the course, Uncle Ray said, "Chris, you're quite the man now."

"I don't feel like a man. I feel like a kid."

"But you handle yourself like a man. You've come a long way. You're ready to handle yourself on your own."

"I'm not sure which college I want to go to. It's great to have an offer. I have time to think about it."

"There may be more."

"Maybe."

"What do your parents think about all this?"

"They're happy. You know, Uncle Ray, I give you a lot of the credit. You helped me stay on track. I still take that stuff about personal strength and people skills and critical thinking seriously. I have a lot to learn."

"You'll never stop learning, Chris, but you have a head start. You did the work. You could have blown off working on being your best self, but you didn't. You took it seriously. Now you can use your senior year to prepare for college."

"My construction job has been great, and I'm saving for college."

"Have you decided what you want to do? What you want to major in?"

"I'm not sure. But I've been thinking about engineering. I might like to be a builder."

"There's a lot of money in construction."

"I know. Mr. Winchester's been telling me about it."

"So what are you doing when you're not working? Are you dating anyone special now?"

Chris shook his head. "I don't have time for that, Uncle Ray. I used to have a girlfriend, but I found out I don't like being tied down. She was nice, but she wanted me to do this and do that. I didn't like it."

"And your plate is full."

Chris laughed. "Yeah, my plate is full."

"I'll tell you a secret. Your plate is always going to be full. The thing is, you've handled it well so far. You think ahead. You make good choices. You're taking charge of your life. I'm proud of what you've accomplished."

"I've done some dumb things, too, Uncle Ray."

"I'm sure you have. But I bet you learned from your mistakes, right?"

"I guess I have. I try not to make the same mistake twice."

"You've really come a long way. You're still growing, but you're on track. I just want you to know I'll always be there for you. You da man, Chris. You da man."

"Thanks, Uncle Ray."

———————— ❖ ————————

"I still take that stuff about personal strength and people skills and critical thinking seriously. I have a lot to learn."

———————— ❖ ————————

Uncle Ray Says

If you've read this far, then you know Uncle Ray is the kind of guy who tells it like it is. Of course, there's more to a relationship than can be told in a book like this. A lot more would have happened and a lot more would have been said. Here's a sample of the kind of things Uncle Ray would tell Chris from time to time...

About learning...

As a teenager, your mission in life is to prepare yourself to be an adult. You only have about ten or twelve years to do this, so take it seriously. Try to have fun along the way, but remember—you won't get a second chance.

————————— ❖ —————————

Teenagers have a full plate. They have a lot to learn to make it on their own as adult—more than they realize. By the time they're adults, most people have learned only about a tenth of what they need to know. They may try to catch up, but many never do. Kids who work on personal development during their teens end up with an amazing edge.

————————— ❖ —————————

Here's what teens need to work on—personal strength, people skills, critical thinking skills, life skills, and formal education. Not to mention health and fitness and service and spirituality. That's a full plate. Later, as adults, they'll need to learn about the business they're in. But success as an adult depends on how strong you are in all these areas.

❖

The most important item on your plate is exercising personal strength. Work on being a stronger version of the good person you already are.

❖

Another huge item on your plate is critical thinking skills. You need to exercise judgment to control your impulses and to create a foundation for thinking logically. The window for building this foundation opens at puberty and closes in your early twenties. It's a use it or lose it deal, with enormous consequences.

❖

One of the best ways to get smarter is to learn from other smart people. Do more asking than arguing. More listening than talking.

❖

No teenager should be bored. Most of the stuff that will build you up and make you strong is fun and exciting. If you're bored, you've lost your way and you're in trouble.

❖

It's great to find something you really care about. Maybe it's a sport. Or your church. Or something like scouting, a hobby or an extracurricular activity. Whatever it is, go with your passion. Do more of it. Get real good at it. Become a leader in it.

———————— ❖ ————————

You may know what to do, but that doesn't mean you can do it. To get good at anything, you need to do it a lot. All those repetitions will wire your brain.

———————— ❖ ————————

Just because something happened to you, it doesn't mean you learned anything from it. If you want the lesson, you have to dig for it. Ask yourself what happened, why did it happen, what were the consequences, and what would you do differently in a similar situation.

———————— ❖ ————————

One of the secrets to getting stronger as a teenager is to make friends with an adult who has something to offer, someone you can talk to. It might be your mom or your dad or another relative. A teacher, a coach, a minister or someone in charge of a youth program. One is good, more is better. Learn as much as you can from these folks.

———————— ❖ ————————

When thinking about a future career, remember that hard work isn't as hard if you love doing it. One of the secrets of life is to find that kind of work and do more of it. It's almost impossible to do anything really well if you don't love doing it.

———————— ❖ ————————

If you want to get ahead, never stop learning. Work on what you know, what you can do, who you are.

———————————❖———————————

About girls...

Some girls are so cute they make your heart beat faster. This is natural, and guys like to compare notes about who's hot and who's not. But don't be fooled. When you get to know a girl, you'll start to see her differently. After the first impression, it's stuff like intelligence and strong character that make a girl seem beautiful. Who she is as a person trumps good looks every time.

———————————❖———————————

Yes, sex is a great thing. But it's also complicated and potentially dangerous, not something you want to fool around with. You need more time to learn about yourself, relationships and women. You need to be ready to handle the risks, responsibilities and the commitment. If you're smart, you'll wait until you're an adult.

———————————❖———————————

When it comes to making out—and more— always honor the girl's wishes. Treat her with respect and kindness. Never push her to do something she says she doesn't want to do.

———————————❖———————————

About friends...

Some kids think it's uncool to be serious and smart. Their idea of coolness is to joke and laugh about everything and fool around a lot. They won't find out until later how wrong they were.

———————— ❖ ————————

When your friends invite you to do something exciting with them, before you go along, think about the consequences. Is this something you'd like your mom or dad to watch you do?

———————— ❖ ————————

The people who treat you badly aren't your friends. If they put you down or say things about you behind your back, they aren't your friends. If this happens to you, find yourself some new friends.

———————— ❖ ————————

About alcohol, drugs, etc...

Some kids think it's fun to use alcohol and drugs. They think getting high and taking risks makes them seem adult. The truth is, these substances impair your judgment at a time when the judgment part of your brain is under construction and vulnerable. Alcohol and drugs can also do permanent damage—limit the growth of that part of your brain. And oh yeah, they're addictive.

———————— ❖ ————————

Smoking isn't cool, either. Get real. It's just an addiction, an expensive one that can lead to cancer and heart disease. What's so cool about that?

———————— ❖ ————————

About parents...

Most teenagers are disappointed when they find out their parents aren't perfect. Well guess what. Nobody has perfect parents. Nobody. So unless your parents are cruel to you, play the cards you were dealt. You don't get to choose your parents, but you do get to choose what kind of a son you'll be.

❖

Teens resent their parents, because parents aren't always sure how to give their kids the freedom and independence they crave. The trick is to keep your composure and make an effort to communicate with them. By your actions, prove to your parents you're responsible and dependable and trustworthy. Earn your freedom one step at a time.

❖

Some teens have parents who give them anything they want—gadgets, clothes, money, even a new car. It's a mistake to envy them. They're being robbed of the chance to learn about responsibility, hard work and striving to overcome challenges—the stuff you need to get stronger. When these kids get to be adults, they may have a hard time being independent and meeting the challenges of life.

❖

About self-worth...

Many of your friends will want you to be like them. To like what they like, and do what they do. But if you want to be unique and special, you have to be yourself.

———————————❖———————————

What does it mean to be a man? It means to be strong in who you are—your character. It means doing the hard thing, the right thing, instead of taking the easy way out.

———————————❖———————————

When you make a mistake, you may feel like beating yourself up about it. Let these feelings go as quickly as you can, and then learn from what happened. Mistakes can make you smarter.

———————————❖———————————

People want to be nice to nice people. So if you want people to like you, treat everyone with respect, kindness and consideration.

———————————❖———————————

A busy life is good, but treat yourself to regular quiet time. Listen to your innermost thoughts, feelings and ideas. You're a smart person, and your brain has a lot it can tell you.

———————————❖———————————

Why Uncle Ray Talks So Much about the Teen Brain — A Brief Technical Explanation

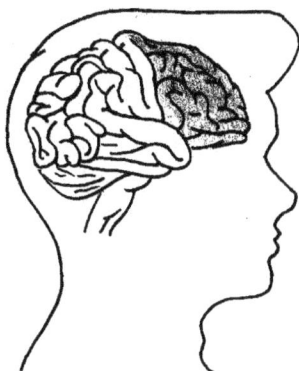

Located behind the forehead, the prefrontal cortex relates perceptions and facts to create meaning. It links cause and effect, so you can foresee future consequences. It's the seat of both creative and logical judgment, as well as both intuitive and rational problem solving. It analyzes, decides, plans, and manages, so a person isn't driven by emotional impulses. Important stuff!

The window for development of the rational decision-making part of the brain opens at puberty and closes ten to twelve years later. "Only the brain cells that fire together will wire together," as brain scientists say. It's also "use it or lose it." The unwired connections will die off, limiting the foundation for intellectual capacity for the rest of adult life. And using critical thinking can help teens stay out of trouble. But because this area is "under construction" during adolescence, it's hard for teens to use it, which accounts for their sometimes impulsive, emotional and risk-taking behavior. Bottom line—teens need to exercise this part of the brain. And because that will be hard for them, adult coaching is crucial.

Personal Strengths

Personal strengths are at the core of who a person is—doing the hard things to deal with adversity and achieve success in life, relationships and work. They're life habits developed over the years through continuous repetition.

One of the smartest things a teen can do is get involved in personal development. A variety of exercises with rich content about personal strengths are available in *ProStar Coach*, an online virtual coaching system for parents and teens developed by the author, Dr. Dennis Coates.

- Acceptance
- Accountability
- Awareness
- Commitment
- Compassion
- Composure
- Cooperation
- Courage
- Creativity
- Decisiveness
- Effort
- Empowerment
- Excellence
- Fairness
- Flexibility
- Focus
- Gratitude
- Honesty
- Initiative
- Integrity
- Intuition
- Loyalty
- Open-mindedness
- Optimism
- Passion
- Patience
- Perseverance
- Proactivity
- Rationality
- Responsibility
- Self-awareness
- Self-confidence

- Self-development
- Self-discipline
- Self-esteem
- Service

- Thoroughness
- Tolerance
- Trust
- Vision

People Skills

People skills are best practices for effective person-to-person communication. Because learning these skills is almost never addressed in high school or college, people learn how to deal with each other in a haphazard way. Hence, ineffective ways of dealing with people often cause problems in life and work relationships.

There are dozens of people skills and a proven, effective way to use each of them. Learning some of these basic skills during the teen years not only helps young people form successful relationships with friends, parents, and other adults, it prevents having to unlearn and relearn these skills later in adult life.

Here is a starter set of basic people skills for teens.

- Listening
- Giving praise
- Giving constructive feedback
- Accepting feedback
- Resolving interpersonal conflicts
- Engaging in dialogue
- Giving encouragement

This is also a good starter set for parents who haven't had people skills training. How-to videos for these communication skills and more than a dozen others are available in *ProStar Coach*, the online virtual coaching system for teens developed by the author, Dr. Dennis Coates.

More Resources for Teens

After Conversations with the Wise Uncle, read this next:

Sean Covey, *The 6 Most Important Decisions You'll Ever Make* (2004). Covey's colorful presentation and light-hearted, conversational style is perfect for teens, and his advice is consistently on target. It contains an abundance of stories from real life and anecdotes from teens. I also recommend his book, *The 7 Habits of Highly Effective Teens* (1998).

Other excellent resources:

- Michael F. Roizen, MD, and others, *You, The Owner's Manual for Teens: A Guide to a Healthy Body and Happy Life* (2011). A virtual encyclopedia of advice from a panel of doctors.
- Pamela Espeland, *Life Lists for Teens: Tips, Steps, Hints and How-tos for Growing Up, Getting Along, Learning and Having Fun* (2003). Dozens of how-tos and tips in the form of lists.
- Chad Foster, *Teenagers Preparing for the Real World* (1999). Straightforward success advice based on personal experience.
- Roger Leslie, *Success Express for Teens: 50 Activities That Will Change Your Life*

2004). Personal development exercises for teens.

- *ProStar Coach* (www.prostarcoach.com). An online virtual coaching service for developing personal strengths and people skills.

A Resource for Adults

Embedded in **Conversations with the Wise Uncle** are insights that can make a huge difference in one's life. An excellent way to make sure they are considered and related to a young person's life, the book may be read one chapter at a time, followed by a discussion with an adult after each chapter. The adult could be a parent, instructor, counselor, coach or other mentor.

To help the adult lead the discussions, Dr. Coates has created a resource called **Learning from the Wise Uncle**. It features discussion guides for each chapter of the book, including discussion questions and main points. The resource also includes worksheets for the teen. The book is available in PDF format to make it easy to print the discussion guides and reader worksheets.

Learning from the Wise Uncle is available as a FREE download at http://www.wiseauntwiseuncle.com.

Acknowledgements

I'd like to thank my old friend, Jack Pryor, whose stories about his teen years inspired me to write this book. I owe an equal debt of thanks to many other people (you know who you are) who took the time to share their teen journey stories.

This book probably wouldn't have been written if I hadn't been encouraged by my business partners to work on it.

I've been greatly influenced by suggestions from people who read early drafts, including Kathleen Scott, Meredith Bell, Debbie Pryor, Teller Coates, Bill Lampton, Patrick Barrett, Cory Richardson-Lauve, and Paula Schlauch. Paula also worked out the production details of the first version of the book.

In addition, throughout the writing I've been inspired by the work of:

- Dr. David Walsh, who more than anyone we know has described the significance of teen brain development and translated this knowledge into advice for parents.
- Dr. John Rosemond's reality-based approach to parenting teens.
- Dr. Kenneth Blanchard, whose popular books about management assured me that this kind of brief, story-based approach can have a profound impact.
- Sean Covey's outstanding books for teens.

About the Author

Dr. Dennis Coates has been CEO of Performance Support Systems, Inc., since 1987. In 1988 he developed *MindFrames*, a personality assessment based on cognitive neuroscience. In 1994 he created *20/20 Insight,* an online multi-source behavior feedback system, used by millions of people worldwide. He is also the creator of *ProStar Coach,* an online virtual coaching service for developing personal strengths and people skills. He writes about learning, personal development and parenting teens. His website: www.howtoraiseateenager.com.

ProStar Coach was originally created for success-oriented young adults, managers, high-performing people in the workplace, consultants to organizations, entrepreneurs and individuals who are trying to give themselves an edge to achieve their goals. Because of its rich content in the area of personal strengths and people skills, along with its emphasis on engaging critical thinking in learning exercises and changing behavior patterns, it's also an outstanding personal development tool for teens. To find out more about *ProStar Coach*, go to www.prostarcoach.com.